The Complete

COSORI

AIR FRYER

COOKBOOK

200+ Easy Nutritious Tasty Recipes
for Your Cosori Air Fryer

EDDA KIRKLAND

CONTENTS

INTRODUCTION

Realizing the Cosori Air Fryer

Most air fryers have the same basic construction. There is a fan at the top that blows down through a heating element. The food is kept in a basket similar to what you would use in a deep fryer. The air circulates down through the basket and all around and through the food, cooking it on all sides.

Below the basket there is a dip tray, that has some sort of unevenly shaped surface. The purpose of the dip tray is to recirculate the air back up and through the air fryer. Air fryers do not have an oil reservoir like you would find in a deep fryer, instead you would at little or no oil to the food before placing it in the basket.

So, technically you are baking your food when you use an air fryer. The reason it is still referred to as a fryer is because it still can produce a crispy fried-like surface on foods. An air fryer can sear foods because of the high temperature of the air that passes through it. They cook at about 392°F. This high temperature is high enough to produce the Maillard Effect. This is the same effect that causes foods to brown and crisp when fried or seared. This is what gives food cooked in an air fryer the almost fried coating.

Significant Advantages of the Cosori Air Fryer

1. Cuts cooking time in half from oven cooking time.

In a test, using an air fryer, at 375°, you could have chicken drumsticks ready inside of 30 minutes. In a conventional oven at about 350°, you would need to bake for 1 hour, turning the pieces halfway through.

Thus, the air fryer can save you up to 50% of the time it would take to cook the same items in an oven. That's not even counting the time needed to preheat your oven.

2. Fries food with as little as 1 tablespoon of oil.

Most fried recipes for an air fryer call for 1 tablespoon of oil or just a few sprays of spray oil.

By comparison in a deep fryer, your food would be immersed in many cups of oil or even pan-fried you would still use up to a cup of oil.

3. You can cook many items with no oil.

The air fryer is a pro at baking and desserts and MANY recipes call for no added oil whatsoever.

4. Parts can go right in the dishwasher.

Air fryer baskets pull right out of the dishwasher and can be quickly rinsed of debris and then go right in the dishwasher. Clean up can literally take under a minute.

5. Doesn't heat up the kitchen like an oven.

In the heat of the summer, even the best-insulated house can still heat up when you crank the oven up for dinnertime. By comparison, the air fryer puts out no ambient heat at all. The unit itself is just slightly warm to the touch on the outside when it's cooking.

6. Doesn't smell up the kitchen like a deep fryer.

Deep fryers cook your food at high heat and since they are typically open on the top and put out a lot of heat and smells, after a quick fry, your whole house often smells of fried foods.

If you fried up some fish tacos, that smell could be much worse.

Practical Methods for Using the Cosori Air Fryer

1) Set up air fryer in your kitchen: Try to place the air fryer on the heat-resistant counter-top. Then ensure five inches distance with the exhaust vent of the kitchen.
2) Pre-heat air fryer: Before starting to cook or make anything preheat the air fryer according to your need and set the timer for 2 or 3 minutes. It will prepare the air fryer ready for making foods.
3) Get a kitchen spray bottle: Spraying oil on the food is simple and easy. It also uses less oil on the food compared to drizzling and brushing. Don't use aerosol spray can on the air fryer basket.
4) Use an aluminum foil sling: To avoid the hassle of using air fryer accessories you can easily use a piece of aluminum foil. You need to place the cake pan or baking dish on the foil. Then, by holding the ends of the foil, it will be easy for you to lift the pan or dish and place it into the air fryer basket.
5) Use the breading technique. Breading is important for many air fryer recipes. Don't skip! All the foods need to coat with flour first, then egg and breadcrumbs. Use the breadcrumbs efficiently and press them onto the food with your hands. Because the powerful fan of the air fryer can blow off the breading.

Useful Tips For Caring for the Cosori Air Fryer

1. Give your food the room it needs

Like many cooking techniques, air-frying needs room to do its thing. Leave space in your basket so there's plenty of space for air to circulate around the food. Overcrowding will make your food take longer to cook and not as crispy.

2. Grease your basket

Dab a little oil on a paper towel and wipe it over the basket to help keep breaded items from sticking. Aerosol sprays aren't recommended directly on the baskets; they can cause the nonstick coating to peel off over time.

3. Avoid cooking super small items

Because of the intense heat and air that an air fryer uses, cutting foods too small can make them easily burn or fly around and get caught in the air fryer. Stick with average bite-sized cuts.

4. Make sure battered foods are as dry as possible

A lot of fried items have a wet coating that won't work well in air fryers; the batter will likely drip off before it cooks. We love panko bread crumbs for the air fryer. Panko provides a dehydrated surface to get nice and toasty in the hot air storm without turning sawdust-dry. (Bonus: It also acts as a barrier, preventing any leaking or dripping during the fry.)

5. Air fry your leftovers

Let's face it: The microwave usually zaps life—and crispy textures—from leftovers. The air fryer will revitalize leftover pizza or roast vegetables much quicker than the oven can.

BEEF , PORK & LAMB RECIPES

Mustard-crusted Rib-eye

Servings: 2
Cooking Time: 9 Minutes

Ingredients:

* Two 6-ounce rib-eye steaks, about 1-inch thick
* 1 teaspoon coarse salt
* ½ teaspoon coarse black pepper
* 2 tablespoons Dijon mustard

Directions:

1. Rub the steaks with the salt and pepper. Then spread the mustard on both sides of the steaks. Cover with foil and let the steaks sit at room temperature for 30 minutes.
2. Preheat the air fryer to 390°F.
3. Cook the steaks for 9 minutes. Check for an internal temperature of 140°F and immediately remove the steaks and let them rest for 5 minutes before slicing.

Rib Eye Cheesesteaks With Fried Onions

Servings: 2
Cooking Time: 20 Minutes

Ingredients:

* 1 (12-ounce) rib eye steak
* 2 tablespoons Worcestershire sauce
* salt and freshly ground black pepper
* ½ onion, sliced
* 2 tablespoons butter, melted
* 4 ounces sliced Cheddar or provolone cheese
* 2 long hoagie rolls, lightly toasted

Directions:

1. Place the steak in the freezer for 30 minutes to make it easier to slice. When it is well-chilled, thinly slice the steak against the grain and transfer it to a bowl. Pour the Worcestershire sauce over the steak and season it with salt and pepper. Allow the meat to come to room temperature.
2. Preheat the air fryer to 400°F.
3. Toss the sliced onion with the butter and transfer it to the air fryer basket. Air-fry at 400°F for 12 minutes, shaking the basket a few times during the cooking process. Place the steak on top of the onions and air-fry for another 6 minutes, stirring the meat and onions together halfway through the cooking time.
4. When the air fryer has finished cooking, divide the steak and onions in half in the air fryer basket, pushing each half to one side of the air fryer basket. Place the cheese on top of each half, push the drawer back into the turned off air fryer and let it sit for 2 minutes, until the cheese has melted.
5. Transfer each half of the cheesesteak mixture into a toasted roll with the cheese side up and dig in!

Marinated Rib-eye Steak With Herb Roasted Mushrooms

Servings: 2
Cooking Time: 10-15 Minutes

Ingredients:

* 2 tablespoons Worcestershire sauce
* ¼ cup red wine
* 2 (8-ounce) boneless rib-eye steaks
* coarsely ground black pepper

- 8 ounces baby bella (cremini) mushrooms, stems trimmed and caps halved
- 2 tablespoons olive oil
- 1 teaspoon dried parsley
- 1 teaspoon fresh thyme leaves
- salt and freshly ground black pepper
- chopped fresh chives or parsley

Directions:

1. Combine the Worcestershire sauce and red wine in a shallow baking dish. Add the steaks to the marinade, pierce them several times with the tines of a fork or a meat tenderizer and season them generously with the coarsely ground black pepper. Flip the steaks over and pierce the other side in a similar fashion, seasoning again with the coarsely ground black pepper. Marinate the steaks for 2 hours.

2. Preheat the air fryer to 400°F.

3. Toss the mushrooms in a bowl with the olive oil, dried parsley, thyme, salt and freshly ground black pepper. Transfer the steaks from the marinade to the air fryer basket, season with salt and scatter the mushrooms on top.

4. Air-fry the steaks for 10 minutes for medium-rare, 12 minutes for medium, or 15 minutes for well-done, flipping the steaks once halfway through the cooking time.

5. Serve the steaks and mushrooms together with the chives or parsley sprinkled on top. A good steak sauce or some horseradish would be a nice accompaniment.

Mustard And Rosemary Pork Tenderloin With Fried Apples

Servings: 2

Cooking Time: 26 Minutes

Ingredients:

- 1 pork tenderloin (about 1-pound)
- 2 tablespoons coarse brown mustard
- salt and freshly ground black pepper
- 1½ teaspoons finely chopped fresh rosemary, plus sprigs for garnish
- 2 apples, cored and cut into 8 wedges
- 1 tablespoon butter, melted
- 1 teaspoon brown sugar

Directions:

1. Preheat the air fryer to 370°F.

2. Cut the pork tenderloin in half so that you have two pieces that fit into the air fryer basket. Brush the mustard onto both halves of the pork tenderloin and then season with salt, pepper and the fresh rosemary. Place the pork tenderloin halves into the air fryer basket and air-fry for 10 minutes. Turn the pork over and air-fry for an additional 8 minutes or until the internal temperature of the pork registers 155°F on an instant read thermometer. If your pork tenderloin is especially thick, you may need to add a minute or two, but it's better to check the pork and add time, than to overcook it.

3. Let the pork rest for 5 minutes. In the meantime, toss the apple wedges with the butter and brown sugar and air-fry at 400°F for 8 minutes, shaking the basket once or twice during the cooking process so the apples cook and brown evenly.

4. Slice the pork on the bias. Serve with the fried apples scattered over the top and a few sprigs of rosemary as garnish.

Lamb Chops

Servings: 2
Cooking Time: 20 Minutes

Ingredients:

- 2 teaspoons oil
- ½ teaspoon ground rosemary
- ½ teaspoon lemon juice
- 1 pound lamb chops, approximately 1-inch thick
- salt and pepper
- cooking spray

Directions:

1. Mix the oil, rosemary, and lemon juice together and rub into all sides of the lamb chops. Season to taste with salt and pepper.
2. For best flavor, cover lamb chops and allow them to rest in the fridge for 20 minutes.
3. Spray air fryer basket with nonstick spray and place lamb chops in it.
4. Cook at 360°F for approximately 20minutes. This will cook chops to medium. The meat will be juicy but have no remaining pink. Cook for a minute or two longer for well done chops. For rare chops, stop cooking after about 12minutes and check for doneness.

Red Curry Flank Steak

Servings: 4
Cooking Time: 18 Minutes

Ingredients:

- 3 tablespoons red curry paste
- ¼ cup olive oil
- 2 teaspoons grated fresh ginger
- 2 tablespoons soy sauce
- 2 tablespoons rice wine vinegar
- 3 scallions, minced
- 1½ pounds flank steak
- fresh cilantro (or parsley) leaves

Directions:

1. Mix the red curry paste, olive oil, ginger, soy sauce, rice vinegar and scallions together in a bowl. Place the flank steak in a shallow glass dish and pour half the marinade over the steak. Pierce the steak several times with a fork or meat tenderizer to let the marinade penetrate the meat. Turn the steak over, pour the remaining marinade over the top and pierce the steak several times again. Cover and marinate the steak in the refrigerator for 6 to 8 hours.
2. When you are ready to cook, remove the steak from the refrigerator and let it sit at room temperature for 30 minutes.
3. Preheat the air fryer to 400°F.
4. Cut the flank steak in half so that it fits more easily into the air fryer and transfer both pieces to the air fryer basket. Pour the marinade over the steak. Air-fry for 18 minutes, depending on your preferred degree of doneness of the steak (12 minutes = medium rare). Flip the steak over halfway through the cooking time.
5. When your desired degree of doneness has been reached, remove the steak to a cutting board and let it rest for 5 minutes before slicing. Thinly slice the flank steak against the grain of the meat. Transfer the slices to a serving platter, pour any juice from the bottom of the air fryer over the sliced flank steak and sprinkle the fresh cilantro on top.

Orange Glazed Pork Tenderloin

Servings: 3

Cooking Time: 23 Minutes

Ingredients:

- 2 tablespoons brown sugar
- 2 teaspoons cornstarch
- 2 teaspoons Dijon mustard
- ½ cup orange juice
- ½ teaspoon soy sauce*
- 2 teaspoons grated fresh ginger
- ¼ cup white wine
- zest of 1 orange
- 1 pound pork tenderloin
- salt and freshly ground black pepper
- oranges, halved (for garnish)
- fresh parsley or other green herb (for garnish)

Directions:

1. Combine the brown sugar, cornstarch, Dijon mustard, orange juice, soy sauce, ginger, white wine and orange zest in a small saucepan and bring the mixture to a boil on the stovetop. Lower the heat and simmer while you cook the pork tenderloin or until the sauce has thickened.

2. Preheat the air fryer to 370°F.

3. Season all sides of the pork tenderloin with salt and freshly ground black pepper. Transfer the tenderloin to the air fryer basket, bending the pork into a wide "U" shape if necessary to fit in the basket. Air-fry at 370°F for 20 to 23 minutes, or until the internal temperature reaches 145°F. Flip the tenderloin over halfway through the cooking process and baste with the sauce.

4. Transfer the tenderloin to a cutting board and let it rest for 5 minutes. Slice the pork at a slight angle and serve immediately with orange halves and fresh herbs to dress it up. Drizzle any remaining glaze over the top.

Chicken-fried Steak

Servings: 2

Cooking Time: 12 Minutes

Ingredients:

- 1½ cups All-purpose flour
- 2 Large egg(s)
- 2 tablespoons Regular or low-fat sour cream
- 2 tablespoons Worcestershire sauce
- 2 ¼-pound thin beef cube steak(s)
- Vegetable oil spray

Directions:

1. Preheat the air fryer to 400°F.

2. Set up and fill two shallow soup plates or small pie plates on your counter: one for the flour; and one for the egg(s), whisked with the sour cream and Worcestershire sauce until uniform.

3. Dredge a piece of beef in the flour, coating it well on both sides and even along the edge. Shake off any excess; then dip the meat in the egg mixture, coating both sides while retaining the flour on the meat. Let any excess egg mixture slip back into the rest. Dredge the meat in the flour once again, coating all surfaces well. Gently shake off the excess coating and set the steak aside if you're coating another steak or two. Once done, coat the steak(s) on both sides with the vegetable oil spray.

4. Set the steak(s) in the basket. If there's more than one steak, make sure they do not overlap or even touch, although the smallest gap between them is enough to get them crunchy. Air-fry undisturbed for 6 minutes.

5. Use kitchen tongs to pick up one of the steaks. Coat it again on both sides with vegetable oil spray. Turn it upside down and set it back in the basket with that same regard for the space between them in larger batches. Repeat with any

other steaks. Continue air-frying undisturbed for 6 minutes, or until golden brown and crunchy.

6. Use kitchen tongs to transfer the steak(s) to a wire rack. Cool for 5 minutes before serving.

Barbecue-style London Broil

Servings: 5

Cooking Time: 17 Minutes

Ingredients:
- ¾ teaspoon Mild smoked paprika
- ¾ teaspoon Dried oregano
- ¾ teaspoon Table salt
- ¾ teaspoon Ground black pepper
- ¼ teaspoon Garlic powder
- ¼ teaspoon Onion powder
- 1½ pounds Beef London broil (in one piece)
- Olive oil spray

Directions:
1. Preheat the air fryer to 400°F.

2. Mix the smoked paprika, oregano, salt, pepper, garlic powder, and onion powder in a small bowl until uniform.

3. Pat and rub this mixture across all surfaces of the beef. Lightly coat the beef on all sides with olive oil spray.

4. When the machine is at temperature, lay the London broil flat in the basket and air-fry undisturbed for 8 minutes for the small batch, 10 minutes for the medium batch, or 12 minutes for the large batch for medium-rare, until an instant-read meat thermometer inserted into the center of the meat registers 130°F (not USDA-approved). Add 1, 2, or 3 minutes, respectively (based on the size of the cut) for medium, until an instant-read meat thermometer registers 135°F (not USDA-approved). Or add 3, 4, or 5 minutes respectively for medium, until an instant-read meat thermometer registers 145°F (USDA-approved).

5. Use kitchen tongs to transfer the London broil to a cutting board. Let the meat rest for 10 minutes. It needs a long time for the juices to be reincorporated into the meat's fibers. Carve it against the grain into very thin (less than ¼-inch-thick) slices to serve.

Indian Fry Bread Tacos

Servings: 4

Cooking Time: 20 Minutes

Ingredients:
- 1 cup all-purpose flour
- 1½ teaspoons salt, divided
- 1½ teaspoons baking powder
- ¼ cup milk
- ¼ cup warm water
- ½ pound lean ground beef
- One 14.5-ounce can pinto beans, drained and rinsed
- 1 tablespoon taco seasoning
- ½ cup shredded cheddar cheese
- 2 cups shredded lettuce
- ¼ cup black olives, chopped
- 1 Roma tomato, diced
- 1 avocado, diced
- 1 lime

Directions:
1. In a large bowl, whisk together the flour, 1 teaspoon of the salt, and baking powder. Make a well in the center and add in the milk and water. Form a ball and gently knead the dough four times. Cover the bowl with a damp towel, and set aside.

2. Preheat the air fryer to 380°F.

3. In a medium bowl, mix together the ground beef, beans, and taco seasoning. Crumble the meat mixture into the air fryer basket and cook for 5 minutes; toss the meat and cook an additional 2 to 3 minutes, or until cooked fully. Place the cooked meat in a bowl for taco assembly; season with the remaining ½ teaspoon salt as desired.

4. On a floured surface, place the dough. Cut the dough into 4 equal parts. Using a rolling pin, roll out each piece of dough to 5 inches in diameter. Spray the dough with cooking spray and place in the air fryer basket, working in batches as needed. Cook for 3 minutes, flip over, spray with cooking spray, and cook for an additional 1 to 3 minutes, until golden and puffy.

5. To assemble, place the fry breads on a serving platter. Equally divide the meat and bean mixture on top of the fry bread. Divide the cheese, lettuce, olives, tomatoes, and avocado among the four tacos. Squeeze lime over the top prior to serving.

Pretzel-coated Pork Tenderloin

Servings: 4
Cooking Time: 10 Minutes

Ingredients:
- 1 Large egg white(s)
- 2 teaspoons Dijon mustard (gluten-free, if a concern)
- 1½ cups (about 6 ounces) Crushed pretzel crumbs (see the headnote; gluten-free, if a concern)
- 1 pound (4 sections) Pork tenderloin, cut into ¼-pound (4-ounce) sections
- Vegetable oil spray

Directions:
1. Preheat the air fryer to 350°F .

2. Set up and fill two shallow soup plates or small pie plates on your counter: one for the egg white(s), whisked with the mustard until foamy; and one for the pretzel crumbs.

3. Dip a section of pork tenderloin in the egg white mixture and turn it to coat well, even on the ends. Let any excess egg white mixture slip back into the rest, then set the pork in the pretzel crumbs. Roll it several times, pressing gently, until the pork is evenly coated, even on the ends. Generously coat the pork section with vegetable oil spray, set it aside, and continue coating and spraying the remaining sections.

4. Set the pork sections in the basket with at least ¼ inch between them. Air-fry undisturbed for 10 minutes, or until an instant-read meat thermometer inserted into the center of one section registers 145°F.

5. Use kitchen tongs to transfer the pieces to a wire rack. Cool for 3 to 5 minutes before serving.

Zesty London Broil

Servings: 4
Cooking Time: 28 Minutes

Ingredients:
- ⅔ cup ketchup
- ¼ cup honey
- ¼ cup olive oil
- 2 tablespoons apple cider vinegar
- 2 tablespoons Worcestershire sauce
- 2 tablespoons minced onion
- ½ teaspoon paprika
- 1 teaspoon salt
- 1 teaspoon freshly ground black pepper
- 2 pounds London broil, top round or flank steak (about 1-inch thick)

Directions:

1. Combine the ketchup, honey, olive oil, apple cider vinegar, Worcestershire sauce, minced onion, paprika, salt and pepper in a small bowl and whisk together.

2. Generously pierce both sides of the meat with a fork or meat tenderizer and place it in a shallow dish. Pour the marinade mixture over the steak, making sure all sides of the meat get coated with the marinade. Cover and refrigerate overnight.

3. Preheat the air fryer to 400°F.

4. Transfer the London broil to the air fryer basket and air-fry for 28 minutes, depending on how rare or well done you like your steak. Flip the steak over halfway through the cooking time.

5. Remove the London broil from the air fryer and let it rest for five minutes on a cutting board. To serve, thinly slice the meat against the grain and transfer to a serving platter.

Korean-style Lamb Shoulder Chops

Servings: 3

Cooking Time: 28 Minutes

Ingredients:

- ⅓ cup Regular or low-sodium soy sauce or gluten-free tamari sauce
- 1½ tablespoons Toasted sesame oil
- 1½ tablespoons Granulated white sugar
- 2 teaspoons Minced peeled fresh ginger
- 1 teaspoon Minced garlic
- ¼ teaspoon Red pepper flakes
- 3 6-ounce bone-in lamb shoulder chops, any excess fat trimmed
- ⅔ cup Tapioca flour
- Vegetable oil spray

Directions:

1. Put the soy or tamari sauce, sesame oil, sugar, ginger, garlic, and red pepper flakes in a large, heavy zip-closed plastic bag. Add the chops, seal, and rub the marinade evenly over them through the bag. Refrigerate for at least 2 hours or up to 6 hours, turning the bag at least once so the chops move around in the marinade.

2. Set the bag out on the counter as the air fryer heats. Preheat the air fryer to 375°F .

3. Pour the tapioca flour on a dinner plate or in a small pie plate. Remove a chop from the marinade and dredge it on both sides in the tapioca flour, coating it evenly and well. Coat both sides with vegetable oil spray, set it in the basket, and dredge and spray the remaining chop(s), setting them in the basket in a single layer with space between them. Discard the bag with the marinade.

4. Air-fry, turning once, for 25 minutes, or until the chops are well browned and tender when pierced with the point of a paring knife. If the machine is at 360°F, you may need to add up to 3 minutes to the cooking time.

5. Use kitchen tongs to transfer the chops to a wire rack. Cool for just a couple of minutes before serving.

Vietnamese Beef Lettuce Wraps

Servings: 4

Cooking Time: 12 Minutes

Ingredients:

- ⅓ cup low-sodium soy sauce*
- 2 teaspoons fish sauce*
- 2 teaspoons brown sugar
- 1 tablespoon chili paste
- juice of 1 lime
- 2 cloves garlic, minced

- 2 teaspoons fresh ginger, minced
- 1 pound beef sirloin
- Sauce
- ⅓ cup low-sodium soy sauce*
- juice of 2 limes
- 1 tablespoon mirin wine
- 2 teaspoons chili paste
- Serving
- 1 head butter lettuce
- ½ cup julienned carrots
- ½ cup julienned cucumber
- ½ cup sliced radishes, sliced into half moons
- 2 cups cooked rice noodles
- ⅓ cup chopped peanuts

Directions:

1. Combine the soy sauce, fish sauce, brown sugar, chili paste, lime juice, garlic and ginger in a bowl. Slice the beef into thin slices, then cut those slices in half. Add the beef to the marinade and marinate for 1 to 3 hours in the refrigerator. When you are ready to cook, remove the steak from the refrigerator and let it sit at room temperature for 30 minutes.

2. Preheat the air fryer to 400°F.

3. Transfer the beef and marinade to the air fryer basket. Air-fry at 400°F for 12 minutes, shaking the basket a few times during the cooking process.

4. While the beef is cooking, prepare a wrap-building station. Combine the soy sauce, lime juice, mirin wine and chili paste in a bowl and transfer to a little pouring vessel. Separate the lettuce leaves from the head of lettuce and put them in a serving bowl. Place the carrots, cucumber, radish, rice noodles and chopped peanuts all in separate serving bowls.

5. When the beef has finished cooking, transfer it to another serving bowl and invite your guests to build their wraps. To build the wraps, place some beef in a lettuce leaf and top with carrots, cucumbers, some rice noodles and chopped peanuts. Drizzle a little sauce over top, fold the lettuce around the ingredients and enjoy!

Steakhouse Burgers With Red Onion Compote

Servings: 4
Cooking Time: 22 Minutes

Ingredients:

- 1½ pounds lean ground beef
- 2 cloves garlic, minced and divided
- 1 teaspoon Worcestershire sauce
- 1 teaspoon sea salt, divided
- ½ teaspoon black pepper
- 1 tablespoon extra-virgin olive oil
- 1 red onion, thinly sliced
- ¼ cup balsamic vinegar
- 1 teaspoon sugar
- 1 tablespoon tomato paste
- 2 tablespoons mayonnaise
- 2 tablespoons sour cream
- 4 brioche hamburger buns
- 1 cup arugula

Directions:

1. In a large bowl, mix together the ground beef, 1 of the minced garlic cloves, the Worcestershire sauce, ½ teaspoon of the salt, and the black pepper. Form the meat into 1-inch-thick patties. Make a dent in the center (this helps the center cook evenly). Let the meat sit for 15 minutes.

2. Meanwhile, in a small saucepan over medium heat, cook the olive oil and red onion for 4 minutes, stirring frequently to avoid burning.

Add in the balsamic vinegar, sugar, and tomato paste, and cook for an additional 3 minutes, stirring frequently. Transfer the onion compote to a small bowl.

3. Preheat the air fryer to 350°F.

4. In another small bowl, mix together the remaining minced garlic, the mayonnaise, and the sour cream. Spread the mayo mixture on the insides of the brioche buns.

5. Cook the hamburgers for 6 minutes, flip the burgers, and cook an additional 2 to 6 minutes. Check the internal temperature to avoid under- or overcooking. Hamburgers should be cooked to at least 160°F. After cooking, cover with foil and let the meat rest for 5 minutes.

6. Meanwhile, place the buns inside the air fryer and toast them for 3 minutes.

7. To assemble the burgers, place the hamburger on one side of the bun, top with onion compote and ¼ cup arugula, and then place the other half of the bun on top.

Pork Chops

Servings: 2
Cooking Time: 16 Minutes

Ingredients:
- 2 bone-in, centercut pork chops, 1-inch thick (10 ounces each)
- 2 teaspoons Worcestershire sauce
- salt and pepper
- cooking spray

Directions:
1. Rub the Worcestershire sauce into both sides of pork chops.
2. Season with salt and pepper to taste.
3. Spray air fryer basket with cooking spray and place the chops in basket side by side.

4. Cook at 360°F for 16 minutes or until well done. Let rest for 5minutes before serving.

Pork Schnitzel

Servings: 4
Cooking Time: 14 Minutes

Ingredients:
- 4 boneless pork chops, pounded to ¼-inch thickness
- 1 teaspoon salt, divided
- 1 teaspoon black pepper, divided
- ½ cup all-purpose flour
- 2 eggs
- 1 cup breadcrumbs
- ¼ teaspoon paprika
- 1 lemon, cut into wedges

Directions:
1. Season both sides of the pork chops with ½ teaspoon of the salt and ½ teaspoon of the pepper.
2. On a plate, place the flour.
3. In a large bowl, whisk the eggs.
4. In another large bowl, place the breadcrumbs.
5. Season the flour with the paprika and season the breadcrumbs with the remaining ½ teaspoon of salt and ½ teaspoon of pepper.
6. To bread the pork, place a pork chop in the flour, then into the whisked eggs, and then into the breadcrumbs. Place the breaded pork onto a plate and finish breading the remaining pork chops.
7. Preheat the air fryer to 390°F.
8. Place the pork chops into the air fryer, not overlapping and working in batches as needed. Spray the pork chops with cooking spray and cook for 8 minutes; flip the pork and cook for another 4 to 6 minutes or until cooked to an internal temperature of 145°F.
9. Serve with lemon wedges.

Almond And Sun-dried Tomato Crusted Pork Chops

Servings: 4

Cooking Time: 10 Minutes

Ingredients:

- ½ cup oil-packed sun-dried tomatoes
- ½ cup toasted almonds
- ¼ cup grated Parmesan cheese
- ½ cup olive oil
- 2 tablespoons water
- ½ teaspoon salt
- freshly ground black pepper
- 4 center-cut boneless pork chops (about 1¼ pounds)

Directions:

1. Place the sun-dried tomatoes into a food processor and pulse them until they are coarsely chopped. Add the almonds, Parmesan cheese, olive oil, water, salt and pepper. Process all the ingredients into a smooth paste. Spread most of the paste (leave a little in reserve) onto both sides of the pork chops and then pierce the meat several times with a needle-style meat tenderizer or a fork. Let the pork chops sit and marinate for at least 1 hour (refrigerate if marinating for longer than 1 hour).

2. Preheat the air fryer to 370°F.

3. Brush a little olive oil on the bottom of the air fryer basket. Transfer the pork chops into the air fryer basket, spooning a little more of the sun-dried tomato paste onto the pork chops if there are any gaps where the paste may have been rubbed off. Air-fry the pork chops at 370°F for 10 minutes, turning the chops over halfway through the cooking process.

4. When the pork chops have finished cooking, transfer them to a serving plate and serve with mashed potatoes and vegetables for a hearty meal.

Lamb Koftas Meatballs

Servings: 3

Cooking Time: 8 Minutes

Ingredients:

- 1 pound ground lamb
- 1 teaspoon ground cumin
- 1 teaspoon ground coriander
- 2 tablespoons chopped fresh mint
- 1 egg, beaten
- ½ teaspoon salt
- freshly ground black pepper

Directions:

1. Combine all ingredients in a bowl and mix together well. Divide the mixture into 10 portions. Roll each portion into a ball and then by cupping the meatball in your hand, shape it into an oval.

2. Preheat the air fryer to 400°F.

3. Air-fry the koftas for 8 minutes.

4. Serve warm with the cucumber-yogurt dip.

Pork Loin

Servings: 8

Cooking Time: 50 Minutes

Ingredients:

- 1 tablespoon lime juice
- 1 tablespoon orange marmalade
- 1 teaspoon coarse brown mustard
- 1 teaspoon curry powder
- 1 teaspoon dried lemongrass
- 2-pound boneless pork loin roast
- salt and pepper
- cooking spray

Directions:

1. Mix together the lime juice, marmalade, mustard, curry powder, and lemongrass.

2. Rub mixture all over the surface of the pork loin. Season to taste with salt and pepper.

3. Spray air fryer basket with nonstick spray and place pork roast diagonally in basket.

4. Cook at 360°F for approximately 50 minutes, until roast registers 130°F on a meat thermometer.

5. Wrap roast in foil and let rest for 10minutes before slicing.

Italian Meatballs

Servings: 4
Cooking Time: 12 Minutes

Ingredients:

- 12 ounces lean ground beef
- 4 ounces Italian sausage, casing removed
- ½ cup breadcrumbs
- 1 cup grated Parmesan cheese
- 1 egg
- 2 tablespoons milk
- 2 teaspoons Italian seasoning
- ½ teaspoon onion powder
- ½ teaspoon garlic powder
- Pinch of red pepper flakes

Directions:

1. In a large bowl, place all the ingredients and mix well. Roll out 24 meatballs.

2. Preheat the air fryer to 360°F.

3. Place the meatballs in the air fryer basket and cook for 12 minutes, tossing every 4 minutes. Using a food thermometer, check to ensure the internal temperature of the meatballs is 165°F.

Pizza Tortilla Rolls

Servings: 4

Cooking Time: 8 Minutes

Ingredients:

- 1 teaspoon butter
- ½ medium onion, slivered
- ½ red or green bell pepper, julienned
- 4 ounces fresh white mushrooms, chopped
- 8 flour tortillas (6- or 7-inch size)
- ½ cup pizza sauce
- 8 thin slices deli ham
- 24 pepperoni slices (about 1½ ounces)
- 1 cup shredded mozzarella cheese (about 4 ounces)
- oil for misting or cooking spray

Directions:

1. Place butter, onions, bell pepper, and mushrooms in air fryer baking pan. Cook at 390°F for 3minutes. Stir and cook 4 minutes longer until just crisp and tender. Remove pan and set aside.

2. To assemble rolls, spread about 2 teaspoons of pizza sauce on one half of each tortilla. Top with a slice of ham and 3 slices of pepperoni. Divide sautéed vegetables among tortillas and top with cheese.

3. Roll up tortillas, secure with toothpicks if needed, and spray with oil.

4. Place 4 rolls in air fryer basket and cook for 4minutes. Turn and cook 4 minutes, until heated through and lightly browned.

5. Repeat step 4 to cook remaining pizza rolls.

Smokehouse-style Beef Ribs

Servings: 3
Cooking Time: 25 Minutes

Ingredients:
- ¼ teaspoon Mild smoked paprika
- ¼ teaspoon Garlic powder
- ¼ teaspoon Onion powder
- ¼ teaspoon Table salt
- ¼ teaspoon Ground black pepper
- 3 10- to 12-ounce beef back ribs (not beef short ribs)

Directions:
1. Preheat the air fryer to 350°F .
2. Mix the smoked paprika, garlic powder, onion powder, salt, and pepper in a small bowl until uniform. Massage and pat this mixture onto the ribs.
3. When the machine is at temperature, set the ribs in the basket in one layer, turning them on their sides if necessary, sort of like they're spooning but with at least ¼ inch air space between them. Air-fry for 25 minutes, turning once, until deep brown and sizzling.
4. Use kitchen tongs to transfer the ribs to a wire rack. Cool for 5 minutes before serving.

Extra Crispy Country-style Pork Riblets

Servings: 3
Cooking Time: 30 Minutes

Ingredients:
- ⅓ cup Tapioca flour
- 2½ tablespoons Chile powder
- ¾ teaspoon Table salt (optional)
- 1¼ pounds Boneless country-style pork ribs, cut into 1½-inch chunks
- Vegetable oil spray

Directions:
1. Preheat the air fryer to 375°F .
2. Mix the tapioca flour, chile powder, and salt (if using) in a large bowl until well combined. Add the country-style rib chunks and toss well to coat thoroughly.
3. When the machine is at temperature, gently shake off any excess tapioca coating from the chunks. Generously coat them on all sides with vegetable oil spray. Arrange the chunks in the basket in one (admittedly fairly tight) layer. The pieces may touch. Air-fry for 30 minutes, rearranging the pieces at the 10- and 20-minute marks to expose any touching bits, until very crisp and well browned.
4. Gently pour the contents of the basket onto a wire rack. Cool for 5 minutes before serving.

Lollipop Lamb Chops With Mint Pesto

Servings: 4
Cooking Time: 7 Minutes

Ingredients:
- Mint Pesto
- ½ small clove garlic
- ¼ cup packed fresh parsley
- ¾ cup packed fresh mint
- ½ teaspoon lemon juice
- ¼ cup grated Parmesan cheese
- ⅓ cup shelled pistachios
- ¼ teaspoon salt
- ½ cup olive oil
- 8 "frenched" lamb chops (1 rack)
- olive oil
- salt and freshly ground black pepper
- 1 tablespoon dried rosemary, chopped

- 1 tablespoon dried thyme

Directions:

1. Make the pesto by combining the garlic, parsley and mint in a food processor and process until finely chopped. Add the lemon juice, Parmesan cheese, pistachios and salt. Process until all the ingredients have turned into a paste. With the processor running, slowly pour the olive oil in through the feed tube. Scrape the sides of the processor with a spatula and process for another 30 seconds.

2. Preheat the air fryer to 400°F.

3. Rub both sides of the lamb chops with olive oil and season with salt, pepper, rosemary and thyme, pressing the herbs into the meat gently with your fingers. Transfer the lamb chops to the air fryer basket.

4. Air-fry the lamb chops at 400°F for 5 minutes. Flip the chops over and air-fry for an additional 2 minutes. This should bring the chops to a medium-rare doneness, depending on their thickness. Adjust the cooking time up or down a minute or two accordingly for different degrees of doneness.

5. Serve the lamb chops with mint pesto drizzled on top.

POULTRY RECIPES

Lemon Sage Roast Chicken

Servings: 4
Cooking Time: 60 Minutes

Ingredients:
- 1 (4-pound) chicken
- 1 bunch sage, divided
- 1 lemon, zest and juice
- salt and freshly ground black pepper

Directions:
1. Preheat the air fryer to 350°F and pour a little water into the bottom of the air fryer drawer. (This will help prevent the grease that drips into the bottom drawer from burning and smoking.)
2. Run your fingers between the skin and flesh of the chicken breasts and thighs. Push a couple of sage leaves up underneath the skin of the chicken on each breast and each thigh.
3. Push some of the lemon zest up under the skin of the chicken next to the sage. Sprinkle some of the zest inside the chicken cavity, and reserve any leftover zest. Squeeze the lemon juice all over the chicken and in the cavity as well.
4. Season the chicken, inside and out, with the salt and freshly ground black pepper. Set a few sage leaves aside for the final garnish. Crumple up the remaining sage leaves and push them into the cavity of the chicken, along with one of the squeezed lemon halves.
5. Place the chicken breast side up into the air fryer basket and air-fry for 20 minutes at 350°F. Flip the chicken over so that it is breast side down and continue to air-fry for another 20 minutes. Return the chicken to breast side up and finish air-frying for 20 more minutes. The internal temperature of the chicken should register 165°F in the thickest part of the thigh when fully cooked. Remove the chicken from the air fryer and let it rest on a cutting board for at least 5 minutes.
6. Cut the rested chicken into pieces, sprinkle with the reserved lemon zest and garnish with the reserved sage leaves.

Chicken Wellington

Servings: 2
Cooking Time: 31 Minutes

Ingredients:
- 2 (5-ounce) boneless, skinless chicken breasts
- ½ cup White Worcestershire sauce
- 3 tablespoons butter
- ½ cup finely diced onion (about ½ onion)
- 8 ounces button mushrooms, finely chopped
- ¼ cup chicken stock
- 2 tablespoons White Worcestershire sauce (or white wine)
- salt and freshly ground black pepper
- 1 tablespoon chopped fresh tarragon
- 2 sheets puff pastry, thawed
- 1 egg, beaten
- vegetable oil

Directions:
1. Place the chicken breasts in a shallow dish. Pour the White Worcestershire sauce over the chicken coating both sides and marinate for 30 minutes.
2. While the chicken is marinating, melt the butter in a large skillet over medium-high heat on the stovetop. Add the onion and sauté for a few minutes, until it starts to soften. Add the

mushrooms and sauté for 5 minutes until the vegetables are brown and soft. Deglaze the skillet with the chicken stock, scraping up any bits from the bottom of the pan. Add the White Worcestershire sauce and simmer for 3 minutes until the mixture reduces and starts to thicken. Season with salt and freshly ground black pepper. Remove the mushroom mixture from the heat and stir in the fresh tarragon. Let the mushroom mixture cool.

3.   Preheat the air fryer to 360°F.

4.   Remove the chicken from the marinade and transfer it to the air fryer basket. Tuck the small end of the chicken breast under the thicker part to shape it into a circle rather than an oval. Pour the marinade over the chicken and air-fry for 10 minutes.

5.   Roll out the puff pastry and cut out two 6-inch squares. Brush the perimeter of each square with the egg wash. Place half of the mushroom mixture in the center of each puff pastry square. Place the chicken breasts, top side down on the mushroom mixture. Starting with one corner of puff pastry and working in one direction, pull the pastry up over the chicken to enclose it and press the ends of the pastry together in the middle. Brush the pastry with the egg wash to seal the edges. Turn the Wellingtons over and set aside.

6.   To make a decorative design with the remaining puff pastry, cut out four 10-inch strips. For each Wellington, twist two of the strips together, place them over the chicken breast wrapped in puff pastry, and tuck the ends underneath to seal it. Brush the entire top and sides of the Wellingtons with the egg wash.

7.   Preheat the air fryer to 350°F.

8.   Spray or brush the air fryer basket with vegetable oil. Air-fry the chicken Wellingtons for 13 minutes. Carefully turn the Wellingtons over. Air-fry for another 8 minutes. Transfer to serving plates, light a candle and enjoy!

Chicken Chimichangas

Servings: 4
Cooking Time: 10 Minutes

Ingredients:
- 2 cups cooked chicken, shredded
- 2 tablespoons chopped green chiles
- ½ teaspoon oregano
- ½ teaspoon cumin
- ½ teaspoon onion powder
- ¼ teaspoon garlic powder
- salt and pepper
- 8 flour tortillas (6- or 7-inch diameter)
- oil for misting or cooking spray
- Chimichanga Sauce
- 2 tablespoons butter
- 2 tablespoons flour
- 1 cup chicken broth
- ¼ cup light sour cream
- ¼ teaspoon salt
- 2 ounces Pepper Jack or Monterey Jack cheese, shredded

Directions:
1. Make the sauce by melting butter in a saucepan over medium-low heat. Stir in flour until smooth and slightly bubbly. Gradually add broth, stirring constantly until smooth. Cook and stir 1 minute, until the mixture slightly thickens. Remove from heat and stir in sour cream and salt. Set aside.

2. In a medium bowl, mix together the chicken, chiles, oregano, cumin, onion powder, garlic, salt,

and pepper. Stir in 3 to 4 tablespoons of the sauce, using just enough to make the filling moist but not soupy.

3. Divide filling among the 8 tortillas. Place filling down the center of tortilla, stopping about 1 inch from edges. Fold one side of tortilla over filling, fold the two sides in, and then roll up. Mist all sides with oil or cooking spray.

4. Place chimichangas in air fryer basket seam side down. To fit more into the basket, you can stand them on their sides with the seams against the sides of the basket.

5. Cook at 360°F for 10 minutes or until heated through and crispy brown outside.

6. Add the shredded cheese to the remaining sauce. Stir over low heat, warming just until the cheese melts. Don't boil or sour cream may curdle.

7. Drizzle the sauce over the chimichangas.

Crispy "fried" Chicken

Servings: 4
Cooking Time: 14 Minutes

Ingredients:

- ¾ cup all-purpose flour
- ½ teaspoon paprika
- ¼ teaspoon black pepper
- ¼ teaspoon salt
- 2 large eggs
- 1½ cups panko breadcrumbs
- 1 pound boneless, skinless chicken tenders

Directions:

1. Preheat the air fryer to 400°F.
2. In a shallow bowl, mix the flour with the paprika, pepper, and salt.
3. In a separate bowl, whisk the eggs; set aside.
4. In a third bowl, place the breadcrumbs.

5. Liberally spray the air fryer basket with olive oil spray.

6. Pat the chicken tenders dry with a paper towel. Dredge the tenders one at a time in the flour, then dip them in the egg, and toss them in the breadcrumb coating. Repeat until all tenders are coated.

7. Set each tender in the air fryer, leaving room on each side of the tender to allow for flipping.

8. When the basket is full, cook 4 to 7 minutes, flip, and cook another 4 to 7 minutes.

9. Remove the tenders and let cool 5 minutes before serving. Repeat until all tenders are cooked.

Chicken Cutlets With Broccoli Rabe And Roasted Peppers

Servings: 2
Cooking Time: 10 Minutes

Ingredients:

- ½ bunch broccoli rabe
- olive oil, in a spray bottle
- salt and freshly ground black pepper
- ⅔ cup roasted red pepper strips
- 2 (4-ounce) boneless, skinless chicken breasts
- 2 tablespoons all-purpose flour*
- 1 egg, beaten
- ⅓ cup seasoned breadcrumbs*
- 2 slices aged provolone cheese

Directions:

1. Bring a medium saucepot of salted water to a boil on the stovetop. Blanch the broccoli rabe for 3 minutes in the boiling water and then drain. When it has cooled a little, squeeze out as much water as possible, drizzle a little olive oil on top, season with salt and black pepper and set aside. Dry the roasted red peppers with a clean kitchen towel and set them aside as well.

2. Place each chicken breast between 2 pieces of plastic wrap. Use a meat pounder to flatten the chicken breasts to about ½-inch thick. Season the chicken on both sides with salt and pepper.

3. Preheat the air fryer to 400°F.

4. Set up a dredging station with three shallow dishes. Place the flour in one dish, the egg in a second dish and the breadcrumbs in a third dish. Coat the chicken on all sides with the flour. Shake off any excess flour and dip the chicken into the egg. Let the excess egg drip off and coat both sides of the chicken in the breadcrumbs. Spray the chicken with olive oil on both sides and transfer to the air fryer basket.

5. Air-fry the chicken at 400°F for 5 minutes. Turn the chicken over and air-fry for another minute. Then, top the chicken breast with the broccoli rabe and roasted peppers. Place a slice of the provolone cheese on top and secure it with a toothpick or two.

6. Air-fry at 360° for 3 to 4 minutes to melt the cheese and warm everything together.

Southwest Gluten-free Turkey Meatloaf

Servings: 8

Cooking Time: 35 Minutes

Ingredients:
- 1 pound lean ground turkey
- ¼ cup corn grits
- ¼ cup diced onion
- 1 teaspoon minced garlic
- ½ teaspoon black pepper
- ½ teaspoon salt
- 1 large egg
- ½ cup ketchup
- 4 teaspoons chipotle hot sauce
- ⅓ cup shredded cheddar cheese

Directions:
1. Preheat the air fryer to 350°F.

2. In a large bowl, mix together the ground turkey, corn grits, onion, garlic, black pepper, and salt.

3. In a small bowl, whisk the egg. Add the egg to the turkey mixture and combine.

4. In a small bowl, mix the ketchup and hot sauce. Set aside.

5. Liberally spray a 9-x-4-inch loaf pan with olive oil spray. Depending on the size of your air fryer, you may need to use 2 or 3 mini loaf pans.

6. Spoon the ground turkey mixture into the loaf pan and evenly top with half of the ketchup mixture. Cover with foil and place the meatloaf into the air fryer. Cook for 30 minutes; remove the foil and discard. Check the internal temperature (it should be nearing 165°F).

7. Coat the top of the meatloaf with the remaining ketchup mixture, and sprinkle the cheese over the top. Place the meatloaf back in the air fryer for the remaining 5 minutes (or until the internal temperature reaches 165°F).

8. Remove from the oven and let cool 5 minutes before serving. Serve warm with desired sides.

Coconut Chicken With Apricot-ginger Sauce

Servings: 4

Cooking Time: 8 Minutes Per Batch

Ingredients:
- 1½ pounds boneless, skinless chicken tenders, cut in large chunks (about 1¼ inches)
- salt and pepper
- ½ cup cornstarch
- 2 eggs

* 1 tablespoon milk
* 3 cups shredded coconut (see below)
* oil for misting or cooking spray
* Apricot-Ginger Sauce
* ½ cup apricot preserves
* 2 tablespoons white vinegar
* ¼ teaspoon ground ginger
* ¼ teaspoon low-sodium soy sauce
* 2 teaspoons white or yellow onion, grated or finely minced

Directions:

1. Mix all ingredients for the Apricot-Ginger Sauce well and let sit for flavors to blend while you cook the chicken.
2. Season chicken chunks with salt and pepper to taste.
3. Place cornstarch in a shallow dish.
4. In another shallow dish, beat together eggs and milk.
5. Place coconut in a third shallow dish. (If also using panko breadcrumbs, as suggested below, stir them to mix well.)
6. Spray air fryer basket with oil or cooking spray.
7. Dip each chicken chunk into cornstarch, shake off excess, and dip in egg mixture.
8. Shake off excess egg mixture and roll lightly in coconut or coconut mixture. Spray with oil.
9. Place coated chicken chunks in air fryer basket in a single layer, close together but without sides touching.
10. Cook at 360°F for 4minutes, stop, and turn chunks over.
11. Cook an additional 4 minutes or until chicken is done inside and coating is crispy brown.
12. Repeat steps 9 through 11 to cook remaining chicken chunks.

Jerk Turkey Meatballs

Servings: 7
Cooking Time: 8 Minutes

Ingredients:

* 1 pound lean ground turkey
* ¼ cup chopped onion
* 1 teaspoon minced garlic
* ½ teaspoon dried thyme
* ¼ teaspoon ground cinnamon
* 1 teaspoon cayenne pepper
* ½ teaspoon paprika
* ½ teaspoon salt
* ⅛ teaspoon black pepper
* ¼ teaspoon red pepper flakes
* 2 teaspoons brown sugar
* 1 large egg, whisked
* ⅓ cup panko breadcrumbs
* 2⅓ cups cooked brown Jasmine rice
* 2 green onions, chopped
* ¾ cup sweet onion dressing

Directions:

1. Preheat the air fryer to 350°F.
2. In a medium bowl, mix the ground turkey with the onion, garlic, thyme, cinnamon, cayenne pepper, paprika, salt, pepper, red pepper flakes, and brown sugar. Add the whisked egg and stir in the breadcrumbs until the turkey starts to hold together.
3. Using a 1-ounce scoop, portion the turkey into meatballs. You should get about 28 meatballs.
4. Spray the air fryer basket with olive oil spray.
5. Place the meatballs into the air fryer basket and cook for 5 minutes, shake the basket, and cook another 2 to 4 minutes (or until the internal temperature of the meatballs reaches 165°F).
6. Remove the meatballs from the basket and repeat for the remaining meatballs.

7. Serve warm over a bed of rice with chopped green onions and spicy Caribbean jerk dressing.

Air-fried Turkey Breast With Cherry Glaze

Servings: 6
Cooking Time: 54 Minutes

Ingredients:
- 1 (5-pound) turkey breast
- 2 teaspoons olive oil
- 1 teaspoon dried thyme
- ½ teaspoon dried sage
- 1 teaspoon salt
- ½ teaspoon freshly ground black pepper
- ½ cup cherry preserves
- 1 tablespoon chopped fresh thyme leaves
- 1 teaspoon soy sauce*
- freshly ground black pepper

Directions:
1. All turkeys are built differently, so depending on the turkey breast and how your butcher has prepared it, you may need to trim the bottom of the ribs in order to get the turkey to sit upright in the air fryer basket without touching the heating element. The key to this recipe is getting the right size turkey breast. Once you've managed that, the rest is easy, so make sure your turkey breast fits into the air fryer basket before you Preheat the air fryer.
2. Preheat the air fryer to 350°F.
3. Brush the turkey breast all over with the olive oil. Combine the thyme, sage, salt and pepper and rub the outside of the turkey breast with the spice mixture.
4. Transfer the seasoned turkey breast to the air fryer basket, breast side up, and air-fry at 350°F for 25 minutes. Turn the turkey breast on its side and air-fry for another 12 minutes. Turn the turkey breast on the opposite side and air-fry for 12 more minutes. The internal temperature of the turkey breast should reach 165°F when fully cooked.
5. While the turkey is air-frying, make the glaze by combining the cherry preserves, fresh thyme, soy sauce and pepper in a small bowl. When the cooking time is up, return the turkey breast to an upright position and brush the glaze all over the turkey. Air-fry for a final 5 minutes, until the skin is nicely browned and crispy. Let the turkey rest, loosely tented with foil, for at least 5 minutes before slicing and serving.

Tandoori Chicken Legs

Servings: 2
Cooking Time: 30 Minutes

Ingredients:
- 1 cup plain yogurt
- 2 cloves garlic, minced
- 1 tablespoon grated fresh ginger
- 2 teaspoons paprika
- 2 teaspoons ground coriander
- 1 teaspoon ground turmeric
- 1 teaspoon salt
- ¼ teaspoon ground cayenne pepper
- juice of 1 lime
- 2 bone-in, skin-on chicken legs
- fresh cilantro leaves

Directions:
1. Make the marinade by combining the yogurt, garlic, ginger, spices and lime juice. Make slashes into the chicken legs to help the marinade penetrate the meat. Pour the marinade over the chicken legs, cover and let the chicken marinate for at least an hour or overnight in the refrigerator.

2. Preheat the air fryer to 380°F.

3. Transfer the chicken legs from the marinade to the air fryer basket, reserving any extra marinade. Air-fry for 15 minutes. Flip the chicken over and pour the remaining marinade over the top. Air-fry for another 15 minutes, watching to make sure it doesn't brown too much. If it does start to get too brown, you can loosely tent the chicken with aluminum foil, tucking the ends of the foil under the chicken to stop it from blowing around.

4. Serve over rice with some fresh cilantro on top.

Maple Bacon Wrapped Chicken Breasts

Servings: 2
Cooking Time: 18 Minutes

Ingredients:

- 2 (6-ounce) boneless, skinless chicken breasts
- 2 tablespoons maple syrup, divided
- freshly ground black pepper
- 6 slices thick-sliced bacon
- fresh celery or parsley leaves
- Ranch Dressing:
- ¼ cup mayonnaise
- ¼ cup buttermilk
- ¼ cup Greek yogurt
- 1 tablespoon chopped fresh chives
- 1 tablespoon chopped fresh parsley
- 1 tablespoon chopped fresh dill
- 1 tablespoon lemon juice
- salt and freshly ground black pepper

Directions:

1. Brush the chicken breasts with half the maple syrup and season with freshly ground black pepper. Wrap three slices of bacon around each chicken breast, securing the ends with toothpicks.

2. Preheat the air fryer to 380°F.

3. Air-fry the chicken for 6 minutes. Then turn the chicken breasts over, pour more maple syrup on top and air-fry for another 6 minutes. Turn the chicken breasts one more time, brush the remaining maple syrup all over and continue to air-fry for a final 6 minutes.

4. While the chicken is cooking, prepare the dressing by combining all the dressing ingredients together in a bowl.

5. When the chicken has finished cooking, remove the toothpicks and serve each breast with a little dressing drizzled over each one. Scatter lots of fresh celery or parsley leaves on top.

Gluten-free Nutty Chicken Fingers

Servings: 4
Cooking Time: 10 Minutes

Ingredients:

- ½ cup gluten-free flour
- ½ teaspoon garlic powder
- ¼ teaspoon onion powder
- ¼ teaspoon black pepper
- ¼ teaspoon salt
- 1 cup walnuts, pulsed into coarse flour
- ½ cup gluten-free breadcrumbs
- 2 large eggs
- 1 pound boneless, skinless chicken tenders

Directions:

1. Preheat the air fryer to 400°F.

2. In a medium bowl, mix the flour, garlic, onion, pepper, and salt. Set aside.

3. In a separate bowl, mix the walnut flour and breadcrumbs.

4. In a third bowl, whisk the eggs.

5. Liberally spray the air fryer basket with olive oil spray.

6. Pat the chicken tenders dry with a paper towel. Dredge the tenders one at a time in the flour, then dip them in the egg, and toss them in the breadcrumb coating. Repeat until all tenders are coated.

7. Set each tender in the air fryer, leaving room on each side of the tender to allow for flipping.

8. When the basket is full, cook 5 minutes, flip, and cook another 5 minutes. Check the internal temperature after cooking completes; it should read 165°F. If it does not, cook another 2 to 4 minutes.

9. Remove the tenders and let cool 5 minutes before serving. Repeat until all the tenders are cooked.

Chicken Flautas

Servings: 6
Cooking Time: 8 Minutes

Ingredients:

- 6 tablespoons whipped cream cheese
- 1 cup shredded cooked chicken
- 6 tablespoons mild pico de gallo salsa
- ⅓ cup shredded Mexican cheese
- ½ teaspoon taco seasoning
- Six 8-inch flour tortillas
- 2 cups shredded lettuce
- ½ cup guacamole

Directions:

1. Preheat the air fryer to 370°F.

2. In a large bowl, mix the cream cheese, chicken, salsa, shredded cheese, and taco seasoning until well combined.

3. Lay the tortillas on a flat surface. Divide the cheese-and-chicken mixture into 6 equal portions; then place the mixture in the center of the tortillas, spreading evenly, leaving about 1 inch from the edge of the tortilla.

4. Spray the air fryer basket with olive oil spray. Roll up the flautas and place them edge side down into the basket. Lightly mist the top of the flautas with olive oil spray.

5. Repeat until the air fryer basket is full. You may need to cook these in batches, depending on the size of your air fryer.

6. Cook for 7 minutes, or until the outer edges are browned.

7. Remove from the air fryer basket and serve warm over a bed of shredded lettuce with guacamole on top.

Philly Chicken Cheesesteak Stromboli

Servings: 2
Cooking Time: 28 Minutes

Ingredients:

- ½ onion, sliced
- 1 teaspoon vegetable oil
- 2 boneless, skinless chicken breasts, partially frozen and sliced very thin on the bias (about 1 pound)
- 1 tablespoon Worcestershire sauce
- salt and freshly ground black pepper
- ½ recipe of Blue Jean Chef pizza dough (see page 229), or 14 ounces of store-bought pizza dough
- 1½ cups grated Cheddar cheese
- ½ cup Cheese Whiz® (or other jarred cheese sauce), warmed gently in the microwave
- tomato ketchup for serving

Directions:

1. Preheat the air fryer to 400°F.

2. Toss the sliced onion with oil and air-fry for 8 minutes, stirring halfway through the cooking time. Add the sliced chicken and Worcestershire sauce to the air fryer basket, and toss to evenly distribute the ingredients. Season the mixture with salt and freshly ground black pepper and air-fry for 8 minutes, stirring a couple of times during the cooking process. Remove the chicken and onion from the air fryer and let the mixture cool a little.

3. On a lightly floured surface, roll or press the pizza dough out into a 13-inch by 11-inch rectangle, with the long side closest to you. Sprinkle half of the Cheddar cheese over the dough leaving an empty 1-inch border from the edge farthest away from you. Top the cheese with the chicken and onion mixture, spreading it out evenly. Drizzle the cheese sauce over the meat and sprinkle the remaining Cheddar cheese on top.

4. Start rolling the stromboli away from you and toward the empty border. Make sure the filling stays tightly tucked inside the roll. Finally, tuck the ends of the dough in and pinch the seam shut. Place the seam side down and shape the Stromboli into a U-shape to fit in the air-fry basket. Cut 4 small slits with the tip of a sharp knife evenly in the top of the dough and lightly brush the stromboli with a little oil.

5. Preheat the air fryer to 370°F.

6. Spray or brush the air fryer basket with oil and transfer the U-shaped stromboli to the air fryer basket. Air-fry for 12 minutes, turning the stromboli over halfway through the cooking time. (Use a plate to invert the stromboli out of the air fryer basket and then slide it back into the basket off the plate.)

7. To remove, carefully flip stromboli over onto a cutting board. Let it rest for a couple of minutes before serving. Slice the stromboli into 3-inch pieces and serve with ketchup for dipping, if desired.

Teriyaki Chicken Drumsticks

Servings: 2

Cooking Time: 17 Minutes

Ingredients:

- 2 tablespoons soy sauce*
- ¼ cup dry sherry
- 1 tablespoon brown sugar
- 2 tablespoons water
- 1 tablespoon rice wine vinegar
- 1 clove garlic, crushed
- 1-inch fresh ginger, peeled and sliced
- pinch crushed red pepper flakes
- 4 to 6 bone-in, skin-on chicken drumsticks
- 1 tablespoon cornstarch
- fresh cilantro leaves

Directions:

1. Make the marinade by combining the soy sauce, dry sherry, brown sugar, water, rice vinegar, garlic, ginger and crushed red pepper flakes. Pour the marinade over the chicken legs, cover and let the chicken marinate for 1 to 4 hours in the refrigerator.

2. Preheat the air fryer to 380°F.

3. Transfer the chicken from the marinade to the air fryer basket, transferring any extra marinade to a small saucepan. Air-fry at 380°F for 8 minutes. Flip the chicken over and continue to air-fry for another 6 minutes, watching to make sure it doesn't brown too much.

4. While the chicken is cooking, bring the reserved marinade to a simmer on the stovetop. Dissolve the cornstarch in 2 tablespoons of water and stir this into the saucepan. Bring to a boil to thicken the sauce. Remove the garlic clove and slices of ginger from the sauce and set aside.

5. When the time is up on the air fryer, brush the thickened sauce on the chicken and air-fry for 3 more minutes. Remove the chicken from the air fryer and brush with the remaining sauce.

6. Serve over rice and sprinkle the cilantro leaves on top.

Apricot Glazed Chicken Thighs

Servings: 2

Cooking Time: 22 Minutes

Ingredients:
- 4 bone-in chicken thighs (about 2 pounds)
- olive oil
- 1 teaspoon salt
- ¼ teaspoon freshly ground black pepper
- ½ teaspoon onion powder
- ¾ cup apricot preserves 1½ tablespoons Dijon mustard
- ½ teaspoon dried thyme
- 1 teaspoon soy sauce
- fresh thyme leaves, for garnish

Directions:
1. Preheat the air fryer to 380°F.
2. Brush or spray both the air fryer basket and the chicken with the olive oil. Combine the salt, pepper and onion powder and season both sides of the chicken with the spice mixture.
3. Place the seasoned chicken thighs, skin side down in the air fryer basket. Air-fry for 10 minutes.

4. While chicken is cooking, make the glaze by combining the apricot preserves, Dijon mustard, thyme and soy sauce in a small bowl.

5. When the time is up on the air fryer, spoon half of the apricot glaze over the chicken thighs and air-fry for 2 minutes. Then flip the chicken thighs over so that the skin side is facing up and air-fry for an additional 8 minutes. Finally, spoon and spread the rest of the glaze evenly over the chicken thighs and air-fry for a final 2 minutes. Transfer the chicken to a serving platter and sprinkle the fresh thyme leaves on top.

Chicken Cordon Bleu

Servings: 2

Cooking Time: 16 Minutes

Ingredients:
- 2 boneless, skinless chicken breasts
- ¼ teaspoon salt
- 2 teaspoons Dijon mustard
- 2 ounces deli ham
- 2 ounces Swiss, fontina, or Gruyère cheese
- ⅓ cup all-purpose flour
- 1 egg
- ½ cup breadcrumbs

Directions:
1. Pat the chicken breasts with a paper towel. Season the chicken with the salt. Pound the chicken breasts to 1½ inches thick. Create a pouch by slicing the side of each chicken breast. Spread 1 teaspoon Dijon mustard inside the pouch of each chicken breast. Wrap a 1-ounce slice of ham around a 1-ounce slice of cheese and place into the pouch. Repeat with the remaining ham and cheese.
2. In a medium bowl, place the flour.
3. In a second bowl, whisk the egg.

4. In a third bowl, place the breadcrumbs.

5. Dredge the chicken in the flour and shake off the excess. Next, dip the chicken into the egg and then in the breadcrumbs. Set the chicken on a plate and repeat with the remaining chicken piece.

6. Preheat the air fryer to 360°F.

7. Place the chicken in the air fryer basket and spray liberally with cooking spray. Cook for 8 minutes, turn the chicken breasts over, and liberally spray with cooking spray again; cook another 6 minutes. Once golden brown, check for an internal temperature of 165°F.

Chicken Schnitzel Dogs

Servings: 4

Cooking Time: 10 Minutes

Ingredients:

- ½ cup flour
- ½ teaspoon salt
- 1 teaspoon marjoram
- 1 teaspoon dried parsley flakes
- ½ teaspoon thyme
- 1 egg
- 1 teaspoon lemon juice
- 1 teaspoon water
- 1 cup breadcrumbs
- 4 chicken tenders, pounded thin
- oil for misting or cooking spray
- 4 whole-grain hotdog buns
- 4 slices Gouda cheese
- 1 small Granny Smith apple, thinly sliced
- ½ cup shredded Napa cabbage
- coleslaw dressing

Directions:

1. In a shallow dish, mix together the flour, salt, marjoram, parsley, and thyme.

2. In another shallow dish, beat together egg, lemon juice, and water.

3. Place breadcrumbs in a third shallow dish.

4. Cut each of the flattened chicken tenders in half lengthwise.

5. Dip flattened chicken strips in flour mixture, then egg wash. Let excess egg drip off and roll in breadcrumbs. Spray both sides with oil or cooking spray.

6. Cook at 390°F for 5minutes. Spray with oil, turn over, and spray other side.

7. Cook for 3 to 5minutes more, until well done and crispy brown.

8. To serve, place 2 schnitzel strips on bottom of each hot dog bun. Top with cheese, sliced apple, and cabbage. Drizzle with coleslaw dressing and top with other half of bun.

Sweet-and-sour Chicken

Servings: 6

Cooking Time: 10 Minutes

Ingredients:

- 1 cup pineapple juice
- 1 cup plus 3 tablespoons cornstarch, divided
- ¼ cup sugar
- ¼ cup ketchup
- ¼ cup apple cider vinegar
- 2 tablespoons soy sauce or tamari
- 1 teaspoon garlic powder, divided
- ¼ cup flour
- 1 tablespoon sesame seeds
- ½ teaspoon salt
- ¼ teaspoon ground black pepper
- 2 large eggs
- 2 pounds chicken breasts, cut into 1-inch cubes
- 1 red bell pepper, cut into 1-inch pieces

- 1 carrot, sliced into ¼-inch-thick rounds

Directions:

1. In a medium saucepan, whisk together the pineapple juice, 3 tablespoons of the cornstarch, the sugar, the ketchup, the apple cider vinegar, the soy sauce or tamari, and ½ teaspoon of the garlic powder. Cook over medium-low heat, whisking occasionally as the sauce thickens, about 6 minutes. Stir and set aside while preparing the chicken.

2. Preheat the air fryer to 370°F.

3. In a medium bowl, place the remaining 1 cup of cornstarch, the flour, the sesame seeds, the salt, the remaining ½ teaspoon of garlic powder, and the pepper.

4. In a second medium bowl, whisk the eggs.

5. Working in batches, place the cubed chicken in the cornstarch mixture to lightly coat; then dip it into the egg mixture, and return it to the cornstarch mixture. Shake off the excess and place the coated chicken in the air fryer basket. Spray with cooking spray and cook for 5 minutes, shake the basket, and spray with more cooking spray. Cook an additional 3 to 5 minutes, or until completely cooked and golden brown.

6. On the last batch of chicken, add the bell pepper and carrot to the basket and cook with the chicken.

7. Place the cooked chicken and vegetables into a serving bowl and toss with the sweet-and-sour sauce to serve.

Chicken Strips

Servings: 4
Cooking Time: 8 Minutes

Ingredients:

- 1 pound chicken tenders
- Marinade
- ¼ cup olive oil
- 2 tablespoons water
- 2 tablespoons honey
- 2 tablespoons white vinegar
- ½ teaspoon salt
- ½ teaspoon crushed red pepper
- 1 teaspoon garlic powder
- 1 teaspoon onion powder
- ½ teaspoon paprika

Directions:

1. Combine all marinade ingredients and mix well.

2. Add chicken and stir to coat. Cover tightly and let marinate in refrigerator for 30minutes.

3. Remove tenders from marinade and place them in a single layer in the air fryer basket.

4. Cook at 390°F for 3minutes. Turn tenders over and cook for 5 minutes longer or until chicken is done and juices run clear.

5. Repeat step 4 to cook remaining tenders.

Taquitos

Servings: 12

Cooking Time: 6 Minutes Per Batch

Ingredients:

- 1 teaspoon butter
- 2 tablespoons chopped green onions
- 1 cup cooked chicken, shredded
- 2 tablespoons chopped green chiles
- 2 ounces Pepper Jack cheese, shredded
- 4 tablespoons salsa
- ½ teaspoon lime juice
- ¼ teaspoon cumin
- ½ teaspoon chile powder
- ⅛ teaspoon garlic powder
- 12 corn tortillas
- oil for misting or cooking spray

Directions:

1. Melt butter in a saucepan over medium heat. Add green onions and sauté a minute or two, until tender.

2. Remove from heat and stir in the chicken, green chiles, cheese, salsa, lime juice, and seasonings.

3. Preheat air fryer to 390°F.

4. To soften refrigerated tortillas, wrap in damp paper towels and microwave for 30 to 60 seconds, until slightly warmed.

5. Remove one tortilla at a time, keeping others covered with the damp paper towels. Place a heaping tablespoon of filling into tortilla, roll up and secure with toothpick. Spray all sides with oil or cooking spray.

6. Place taquitos in air fryer basket, either in a single layer or stacked. To stack, leave plenty of space between taquitos and alternate the direction of the layers, 4 on the bottom lengthwise, then 4 more on top crosswise.

7. Cook for 6minutes or until brown and crispy.

8. Repeat steps 6 and 7 to cook remaining taquitos.

9. Serve hot with guacamole, sour cream, salsa or all three!

Tortilla Crusted Chicken Breast

Servings: 2

Cooking Time: 12 Minutes

Ingredients:

- ⅓ cup flour
- 1 teaspoon salt
- 1½ teaspoons chili powder
- 1 teaspoon ground cumin
- freshly ground black pepper
- 1 egg, beaten
- ¾ cup coarsely crushed yellow corn tortilla chips
- 2 (3- to 4-ounce) boneless chicken breasts
- vegetable oil
- ½ cup salsa
- ½ cup crumbled queso fresco
- fresh cilantro leaves
- sour cream or guacamole (optional)

Directions:

1. Set up a dredging station with three shallow dishes. Combine the flour, salt, chili powder, cumin and black pepper in the first shallow dish. Beat the egg in the second shallow dish. Place the crushed tortilla chips in the third shallow dish.

2. Dredge the chicken in the spiced flour, covering all sides of the breast. Then dip the chicken into the egg, coating the chicken completely. Finally, place the chicken into the tortilla chips and press the chips onto the chicken to make sure they adhere to all sides of the breast.

Spray the coated chicken breasts on both sides with vegetable oil.

3. Preheat the air fryer to 380°F.

4. Air-fry the chicken for 6 minutes. Then turn the chicken breasts over and air-fry for another 6 minutes. (Increase the cooking time if you are using chicken breasts larger than 3 to 4 ounces.)

5. When the chicken has finished cooking, serve each breast with a little salsa, the crumbled queso fresco and cilantro as the finishing touch. Serve some sour cream and/or guacamole at the table, if desired.

Chicken Adobo

Servings: 6
Cooking Time: 12 Minutes

Ingredients:
- 6 boneless chicken thighs
- ¼ cup soy sauce or tamari
- ½ cup rice wine vinegar
- 4 cloves garlic, minced
- ⅛ teaspoon crushed red pepper flakes
- ½ teaspoon black pepper

Directions:
1. Place the chicken thighs into a resealable plastic bag with the soy sauce or tamari, the rice wine vinegar, the garlic, and the crushed red pepper flakes. Seal the bag and let the chicken marinate at least 1 hour in the refrigerator.

2. Preheat the air fryer to 400°F.

3. Drain the chicken and pat dry with a paper towel. Season the chicken with black pepper and liberally spray with cooking spray.

4. Place the chicken in the air fryer basket and cook for 9 minutes, turn over at 9 minutes and check for an internal temperature of 165°F, and cook another 3 minutes.

Crispy Chicken Parmesan

Servings: 4
Cooking Time: 12 Minutes

Ingredients:
- 4 skinless, boneless chicken breasts, pounded thin to ¼-inch thickness
- 1 teaspoon salt, divided
- ½ teaspoon black pepper, divided
- 1 cup flour
- 2 eggs
- 1 cup panko breadcrumbs
- ½ teaspoon dried oregano
- ½ cup grated Parmesan cheese

Directions:
1. Pat the chicken breasts with a paper towel. Season the chicken with ½ teaspoon of the salt and ¼ teaspoon of the pepper.

2. In a medium bowl, place the flour.

3. In a second bowl, whisk the eggs.

4. In a third bowl, place the breadcrumbs, oregano, cheese, and the remaining ½ teaspoon of salt and ¼ teaspoon of pepper.

5. Dredge the chicken in the flour and shake off the excess. Dip the chicken into the eggs and then into the breadcrumbs. Set the chicken on a plate and repeat with the remaining chicken pieces.

6. Preheat the air fryer to 360°F.

7. Place the chicken in the air fryer basket and spray liberally with cooking spray. Cook for 8 minutes, turn the chicken breasts over, and cook another 4 minutes. When golden brown, check for an internal temperature of 165°F.

Chicken Chunks

Servings: 4

Cooking Time: 10 Minutes

Ingredients:

- 1 pound chicken tenders cut in large chunks, about 1½ inches
- salt and pepper
- ½ cup cornstarch
- 2 eggs, beaten
- 1 cup panko breadcrumbs
- oil for misting or cooking spray

Directions:

1. Season chicken chunks to your liking with salt and pepper.

2. Dip chicken chunks in cornstarch. Then dip in egg and shake off excess. Then roll in panko crumbs to coat well.

3. Spray all sides of chicken chunks with oil or cooking spray.

4. Place chicken in air fryer basket in single layer and cook at 390°F for 5minutes. Spray with oil, turn chunks over, and spray other side.

5. Cook for an additional 5minutes or until chicken juices run clear and outside is golden brown.

6. Repeat steps 4 and 5 to cook remaining chicken.

APPETIZERS AND SNACKS

Crab Rangoon Dip With Wonton Chips

Servings: 6
Cooking Time: 18 Minutes

Ingredients:
- Wonton Chips:
- 1 (12-ounce) package wonton wrappers
- vegetable oil
- sea salt
- Crab Rangoon Dip:
- 8 ounces cream cheese, softened
- ¾ cup sour cream
- 1 teaspoon Worcestershire sauce
- 1½ teaspoons soy sauce
- 1 teaspoon sesame oil
- ⅛ teaspoon ground cayenne pepper
- ¼ teaspoon salt
- freshly ground black pepper
- 8 ounces cooked crabmeat
- 1 cup grated white Cheddar cheese
- ⅓ cup chopped scallions
- paprika (for garnish)

Directions:
1. Cut the wonton wrappers in half diagonally to form triangles. Working in batches, lay the wonton triangles on a flat surface and brush or spray both sides with vegetable oil.
2. Preheat the air fryer to 370°F.
3. Place about 10 to 12 wonton triangles in the air fryer basket, letting them overlap slightly. Air-fry for just 2 minutes, shaking the basket halfway through the cooking time. Transfer the wonton chips to a large bowl and season immediately with sea salt. (You'll hear the chips start to spin around in the air fryer when they are almost done.) Repeat with the rest of wontons (keeping those fishing hands at bay!).
4. To make the dip, combine the cream cheese, sour cream, Worcestershire sauce, soy sauce, sesame oil, cayenne pepper, salt, and freshly ground black pepper in a bowl. Mix well and then fold in the crabmeat, Cheddar cheese, and scallions.
5. Transfer the dip to a 7-inch ceramic baking pan or shallow casserole dish. Sprinkle paprika on top and cover the dish with aluminum foil. Lower the dish into the air fryer basket using a sling made of aluminum foil (fold a piece of aluminum foil into a strip about 2-inches wide by 24-inches long). Air-fry for 11 minutes. Remove the aluminum foil and air-fry for another 5 minutes to finish cooking and brown the top. Serve hot with the wonton chips.

Fried Cheese Ravioli With Marinara Sauce

Servings: 4
Cooking Time: 7 Minutes

Ingredients:
- 1 pound cheese ravioli, fresh or frozen
- 2 eggs, lightly beaten
- 1 cup plain breadcrumbs
- ½ teaspoon paprika
- ½ teaspoon dried oregano
- ½ teaspoon salt
- grated Parmesan cheese
- chopped fresh parsley

- 1 to 2 cups marinara sauce (jarred or homemade)

Directions:

1. Bring a stockpot of salted water to a boil. Boil the ravioli according to the package directions and then drain. Let the cooked ravioli cool to a temperature where you can comfortably handle them.

2. While the pasta is cooking, set up a dredging station with two shallow dishes. Place the eggs into one dish. Combine the breadcrumbs, paprika, dried oregano and salt in the other dish.

3. Preheat the air fryer to 380°F.

4. Working with one at a time, dip the cooked ravioli into the egg, coating all sides. Then press the ravioli into the breadcrumbs, making sure that all sides are covered. Transfer the ravioli to the air fryer basket, cooking in batches, one layer at a time. Air-fry at 380°F for 7 minutes.

5. While the ravioli is air-frying, bring the marinara sauce to a simmer on the stovetop. Transfer to a small bowl.

6. Sprinkle a little Parmesan cheese and chopped parsley on top of the fried ravioli and serve warm with the marinara sauce on the side for dipping.

Roasted Red Pepper Dip

Servings: 2
Cooking Time: 15 Minutes

Ingredients:
- 2 Medium-size red bell pepper(s)
- 1¾ cups (one 15-ounce can) Canned white beans, drained and rinsed
- 1 tablespoon Fresh oregano leaves, packed
- 3 tablespoons Olive oil
- 1 tablespoon Lemon juice
- ½ teaspoon Table salt
- ½ teaspoon Ground black pepper

Directions:

1. Preheat the air fryer to 400°F.

2. Set the pepper(s) in the basket and air-fry undisturbed for 15 minutes, until blistered and even blackened.

3. Use kitchen tongs to transfer the pepper(s) to a zip-closed plastic bag or small bowl. Seal the bag or cover the bowl with plastic wrap. Set aside for 20 minutes.

4. Peel each pepper, then stem it, cut it in half, and remove all its seeds and their white membranes.

5. Set the pieces of the pepper in a food processor. Add the beans, oregano, olive oil, lemon juice, salt, and pepper. Cover and process until smooth, stopping the machine at least once to scrape down the inside of the canister. Scrape the dip into a bowl and serve warm, or cover and refrigerate for up to 3 days (although the dip tastes best if it's allowed to come back to room temperature).

Cauliflower "tater" Tots

Servings: 6
Cooking Time: 10 Minutes

Ingredients:
- 1 head of cauliflower
- 2 eggs
- ¼ cup all-purpose flour*
- ½ cup grated Parmesan cheese
- 1 teaspoon salt
- freshly ground black pepper
- vegetable or olive oil, in a spray bottle

Directions:

1. Grate the head of cauliflower with a box grater or finely chop it in a food processor. You

should have about 3½ cups. Place the chopped cauliflower in the center of a clean kitchen towel and twist the towel tightly to squeeze all the water out of the cauliflower. (This can be done in two batches to make it easier to drain all the water from the cauliflower.)

2. Place the squeezed cauliflower in a large bowl. Add the eggs, flour, Parmesan cheese, salt and freshly ground black pepper. Shape the cauliflower into small cylinders or "tater tot" shapes, rolling roughly one tablespoon of the mixture at a time. Place the tots on a cookie sheet lined with paper towel to absorb any residual moisture. Spray the cauliflower tots all over with oil.

3. Preheat the air fryer to 400°F.

4. Air-fry the tots at 400°F, one layer at a time for 10 minutes, turning them over for the last few minutes of the cooking process for even browning. Season with salt and black pepper. Serve hot with your favorite dipping sauce.

Cherry Chipotle Bbq Chicken Wings

Servings: 2
Cooking Time: 12 Minutes

Ingredients:

- 1 teaspoon smoked paprika
- ½ teaspoon dry mustard powder
- 1 teaspoon dried oregano
- 1 teaspoon dried thyme
- ½ teaspoon chili powder
- 1 teaspoon salt
- 2 pounds chicken wings
- vegetable oil or spray
- salt and freshly ground black pepper

- 1 to 2 tablespoons chopped chipotle peppers in adobo sauce
- ⅓ cup cherry preserves ¼ cup tomato ketchup

Directions:

1. Combine the first six ingredients in a large bowl. Prepare the chicken wings by cutting off the wing tips and discarding (or freezing for chicken stock). Divide the drumettes from the win-gettes by cutting through the joint. Place the chicken wing pieces in the bowl with the spice mix. Toss or shake well to coat.

2. Preheat the air fryer to 400°F.

3. Spray the wings lightly with the vegetable oil and air-fry the wings in two batches for 10 minutes per batch, shaking the basket halfway through the cooking process. When both batches are done, toss all the wings back into the basket for another 2 minutes to heat through and finish cooking.

4. While the wings are air-frying, combine the chopped chipotle peppers, cherry preserves and ketchup in a bowl.

5. Remove the wings from the air fryer, toss them in the cherry chipotle BBQ sauce and serve with napkins!

Cheesy Tortellini Bites

Servings: 8
Cooking Time: 10 Minutes

Ingredients:

- 1 large egg
- ½ teaspoon black pepper
- ½ teaspoon garlic powder
- 1 teaspoon Italian seasoning
- 12 ounces frozen cheese tortellini
- ½ cup panko breadcrumbs

Directions:

1. Preheat the air fryer to 380°F.
2. Spray the air fryer basket with an olive-oil-based spray.
3. In a medium bowl, whisk the egg with the pepper, garlic powder, and Italian seasoning.
4. Dip the tortellini in the egg batter and then coat with the breadcrumbs. Place each tortellini in the basket, trying not to overlap them. You may need to cook in batches to ensure the even crisp all around.
5. Bake for 5 minutes, shake the basket, and bake another 5 minutes.
6. Remove and let cool 5 minutes. Serve with marinara sauce, ranch, or your favorite dressing.

Fried Dill Pickle Chips

Servings: 4
Cooking Time: 12 Minutes

Ingredients:
*   1 cup All-purpose flour or tapioca flour
*   1 Large egg white(s)
*   1 tablespoon Brine from a jar of dill pickles
*   1 cup Seasoned Italian-style dried bread crumbs (gluten-free, if a concern)
*   2 Large dill pickle(s) (8 to 10 inches long), cut into ½-inch-thick rounds
*   Vegetable oil spray

Directions:
1. Preheat the air fryer to 400°F.
2. Set up and fill three shallow soup plates or small pie plates on your counter: one for the flour, one for the egg white(s) whisked with the pickle brine, and one for the bread crumbs.
3. Set a pickle round in the flour and turn it to coat all sides, even the edge. Gently shake off the excess flour, then dip the round into the egg-white mixture and turn to coat both sides and the edge. Let any excess egg white mixture slip back into the rest, then set the round in the bread crumbs and turn it to coat both sides as well as the edge. Set aside on a cutting board and soldier on, dipping and coating the remaining rounds. Lightly coat the coated rounds on both sides with vegetable oil spray.
4. Set the pickle rounds in the basket in one layer. Air-fry undisturbed for 7 minutes, or until golden brown and crunchy. Cool in the basket for a few minutes before using kitchen tongs to transfer the (still hot) rounds to a serving platter.

Individual Pizzas

Servings: 2
Cooking Time: 7 Minutes

Ingredients:
*   6 ounces Purchased fresh pizza dough (not a prebaked crust)
*   Olive oil spray
*   4½ tablespoons Purchased pizza sauce or purchased pesto
*   ½ cup (about 2 ounces) Shredded semi-firm mozzarella

Directions:
1. Preheat the air fryer to 400°F.
2. Press the pizza dough into a 5-inch circle for a small air fryer, a 6-inch circle for a medium air fryer, or a 7-inch circle for a large machine. Generously coat the top of the dough with olive oil spray.
3. Remove the basket from the machine and set the dough oil side down in the basket. Smear the sauce or pesto over the dough, then sprinkle with the cheese.
4. Return the basket to the machine and air-fry undisturbed for 7 minutes, or until the dough is

puffed and browned and the cheese has melted. (Extra toppings will not increase the cooking time, provided you add no extra cheese.)

5. Remove the basket from the machine and cool the pizza in it for 5 minutes. Use a large nonstick-safe spatula to transfer the pizza from the basket to a wire rack. Cool for 5 minutes more before serving.

Beer Battered Onion Rings

Servings: 2
Cooking Time: 16 Minutes

Ingredients:

- ⅔ cup flour
- ½ teaspoon baking soda
- 1 teaspoon paprika
- 1 teaspoon salt
- ½ teaspoon freshly ground black pepper
- ¾ cup beer
- 1 egg, beaten
- 1½ cups fine breadcrumbs
- 1 large Vidalia onion, peeled and sliced into ½-inch rings
- vegetable oil

Directions:

1. Set up a dredging station. Mix the flour, baking soda, paprika, salt and pepper together in a bowl. Pour in the beer, add the egg and whisk until smooth. Place the breadcrumbs in a cake pan or shallow dish.

2. Separate the onion slices into individual rings. Dip each onion ring into the batter with a fork. Lift the onion ring out of the batter and let any excess batter drip off. Then place the onion ring in the breadcrumbs and shake the cake pan back and forth to coat the battered onion ring. Pat the ring gently with your hands to make sure the breadcrumbs stick and that both sides of the ring are covered. Place the coated onion ring on a sheet pan and repeat with the rest of the onion rings.

3. Preheat the air fryer to 360°F.

4. Lightly spray the onion rings with oil, coating both sides. Layer the onion rings in the air fryer basket, stacking them on top of each other in a haphazard manner.

5. Air-fry for 10 minutes at 360°F. Flip the onion rings over and rotate the onion rings from the bottom of the basket to the top. Air-fry for an additional 6 minutes.

6. Serve immediately with your favorite dipping sauce.

Garlic-herb Pita Chips

Servings: 4
Cooking Time: 6 Minutes

Ingredients:

- ¼ teaspoon dried basil
- ¼ teaspoon marjoram
- ¼ teaspoon ground oregano
- ¼ teaspoon garlic powder
- ¼ teaspoon ground thyme
- ¼ teaspoon salt
- 2 whole 6-inch pitas, whole grain or white
- oil for misting or cooking spray

Directions:

1. Mix all seasonings together.

2. Cut each pita half into 4 wedges. Break apart wedges at the fold.

3. Mist one side of pita wedges with oil. Sprinkle with half of seasoning mix.

4. Turn pita wedges over, mist the other side with oil, and sprinkle with remaining seasonings.

5. Place pita wedges in air fryer basket and cook at 330°F for 2minutes.

6. Shake basket and cook for 2minutes longer. Shake again, and if needed cook for 2 moreminutes, until crisp. Watch carefully because at this point they will cook very quickly.

Middle Eastern Phyllo Rolls

Servings: 6

Cooking Time: 5 Minutes

Ingredients:

- 6 ounces Lean ground beef or ground lamb
- 3 tablespoons Sliced almonds
- 1 tablespoon Chutney (any variety), finely chopped
- ¼ teaspoon Ground cinnamon
- ¼ teaspoon Ground coriander
- ¼ teaspoon Ground cumin
- ¼ teaspoon Ground dried turmeric
- ¼ teaspoon Table salt
- ¼ teaspoon Ground black pepper
- 6 18 × 14-inch phyllo sheets (thawed, if necessary)
- Olive oil spray

Directions:

1. Set a medium skillet over medium heat for a minute or two, then crumble in the ground meat. Cook for 3 minutes, stirring often, or until well browned. Stir in the almonds, chutney, cinnamon, coriander, cumin, turmeric, salt, and pepper until well combined. Remove from the heat, scrape the cooked ground meat mixture into a bowl, and cool for 15 minutes.

2. Preheat the air fryer to 400°F.

3. Place one sheet of phyllo dough on a clean, dry work surface. (Keep the others covered.) Lightly coat it with olive oil spray, then fold it in half by bringing the short ends together. Place about 3 tablespoons of the ground meat mixture along one of the longer edges, then fold both of the shorter sides of the dough up and over the meat to partially enclose it (and become a border along the sheet of dough). Roll the dough closed, coat it with olive oil spray on all sides, and set it aside seam side down. Repeat this filling and spraying process with the remaining phyllo sheets.

4. Set the rolls seam side down in the basket in one layer with some air space between them. Air-fry undisturbed for 5 minutes, or until very crisp and golden brown.

5. Use kitchen tongs to transfer the rolls to a wire rack. Cool for only 2 or 3 minutes before serving hot.

Savory Sausage Balls

Servings: 10

Cooking Time: 8 Minutes

Ingredients:

- 2 cups all-purpose flour
- 1 tablespoon baking powder
- ½ teaspoon garlic powder
- ¼ teaspoon onion powder
- ½ teaspoon salt
- 3 tablespoons milk
- 2½ cups grated pepper jack cheese
- 1 pound fresh sausage, casing removed

Directions:

1. Preheat the air fryer to 370°F.

2. In a large bowl, whisk together the flour, baking powder, garlic powder, onion powder, and salt. Add in the milk, grated cheese, and sausage.

3. Using a tablespoon, scoop out the sausage and roll it between your hands to form a rounded ball. You should end up with approximately 32 balls.

Place them in the air fryer basket in a single layer and working in batches as necessary.

4. Cook for 8 minutes, or until the outer coating turns light brown.

5. Carefully remove, repeating with the remaining sausage balls.

Prosciutto Mozzarella Bites

Servings: 8
Cooking Time: 6 Minutes

Ingredients:
- 8 pieces full-fat mozzarella string cheese
- 8 thin slices prosciutto
- 16 basil leaves

Directions:
1. Preheat the air fryer to 360°F.
2. Cut the string cheese in half across the center, not lengthwise. Do the same with the prosciutto.
3. Place a piece of prosciutto onto a clean workspace. Top the prosciutto with a basil leaf and then a piece of string cheese. Roll up the string cheese inside the prosciutto and secure with a wooden toothpick. Repeat with the remaining cheese sticks.
4. Place the prosciutto mozzarella bites into the air fryer basket and cook for 6 minutes, checking for doneness at 4 minutes.

Scotch Eggs

Servings: 6
Cooking Time: 12 Minutes

Ingredients:
- 7 Large eggs
- 1½ cups Corn flake crumbs (gluten-free, if a concern)
- 1½ pounds Bulk mild or hot breakfast sausage meat (gluten-free, if a concern)
- Vegetable oil spray
- For garnishing Coarse sea salt or kosher salt

Directions:
1. Bring a little more than 1 inch of water to a boil in a large saucepan set over high heat. Meanwhile, prepare a big bowl of ice water.
2. Set 4, 6, or 8 of the eggs in a vegetable steamer basket and lower them into the pot. Cover, reduce the heat to low, and steam for 10 minutes. Drain the eggs into a colander set in the sink, then put them in the ice water. Cool for 10 minutes, then peel the eggs. (Be careful: the whites are set but not the yolks!)
3. Preheat the air fryer to 375°F (or 380°F or 390°F, if one of these is the closest setting).
4. Lay a sheet of plastic wrap on a clean, dry work surface. Place ¼ pound (4 ounces) of the sausage meat in the center of the sheet, then press the sausage into an oval 7 inches long and about 5 inches wide at its widest part. Place a peeled egg in the center of the sausage, then carefully and gently (no awards for speed!) use the plastic wrap to fold the sausage up and around the egg. Remove the plastic wrap, dampen your clean hands, then smooth and seal the sausage over the egg. Repeat with the remaining sausage and eggs, using a fresh sheet of plastic wrap each time.
5. Set up and fill two shallow soup plates or small pie plates on your counter: one with the remaining egg(s) in it, well beaten until uniform, and the other with the corn flake crumbs. Roll the sausage-covered egg in the beaten egg. Let the excess slip back into the rest, then set the coated egg in the corn flake crumbs. Roll the egg in the corn flake crumbs to coat it evenly and well, even on the ends. Set aside, then coat the remaining sausage-covered eggs.

6. Give the crumbed eggs a generous coating of vegetable oil spray. Set them in the basket in one layer and air-fry undisturbed for 12 minutes, or until the coating is well browned. If the air fryer is at 390°F, the Scotch eggs may be done in 10 minutes.

7. Use kitchen tongs to transfer the eggs to a wire rack. Cool for at least 5 minutes or up to 30 minutes before serving. Split the eggs in half, sprinkle them with salt, and relish every bite.

Fried Wontons

Servings: 24
Cooking Time: 6 Minutes

Ingredients:
- 6 ounces Lean ground beef, pork, or turkey
- 1 tablespoon Regular or reduced-sodium soy sauce or tamari sauce
- 1½ teaspoons Minced garlic
- ¾ teaspoon Ground dried ginger
- ½ teaspoon Ground white pepper
- 24 Wonton wrappers (thawed, if necessary)
- Vegetable oil spray

Directions:
1. Preheat the air fryer to 350°F .
2. Stir the ground meat, soy or tamari sauce, garlic, ginger, and white pepper in a bowl until the spices are uniformly distributed in the mixture.
3. Set a small bowl of water on a clean, dry surface or next to a clean, dry cutting board. Set one wonton wrapper on the surface. Dip your clean finger in the water, then run it along the edges of the wrapper. Set 1 teaspoon of the ground meat mixture in the center of the wrapper. Fold it over, corner to corner, to create a filled triangle. Press to seal the edges, then pull the corners on the longest side up and together over the filling to create the classic wonton shape. Press the corners together to seal. Set aside and continue filling and making more filled wontons.
4. Generously coat the filled wontons on all sides with vegetable oil spray. Arrange them in the basket in one layer and air-fry for 6 minutes, shaking the basket gently at the 2- and 4-minute marks to rearrange the wontons (but always making sure they're still in one layer), until golden brown and crisp.
5. Pour the wontons in the basket onto a wire rack or even into a serving bowl. Cool for 2 or 3 minutes (but not much longer) and serve hot.

Halloumi Fries

Servings: 3
Cooking Time: 12 Minutes

Ingredients:
- 1½ tablespoons Olive oil
- 1½ teaspoons Minced garlic
- ⅛ teaspoon Dried oregano
- ⅛ teaspoon Dried thyme
- ⅛ teaspoon Table salt
- ⅛ teaspoon Ground black pepper
- ¾ pound Halloumi

Directions:
1. Preheat the air fryer to 400°F.
2. Whisk the oil, garlic, oregano, thyme, salt, and pepper in a medium bowl.
3. Lay the piece of halloumi flat on a cutting board. Slice it widthwise into ½-inch-thick sticks. Cut each stick lengthwise into ½-inch-thick batons.
4. Put these batons into the olive oil mixture. Toss gently but well to coat.

5. Place the batons in the basket in a single layer. Air-fry undisturbed for 12 minutes, or until lightly browned, particularly at the edges.

6. Dump the fries out onto a wire rack. They may need a little coaxing with a nonstick-safe spatula to come free. Cool for a couple of minutes before serving hot.

Caponata Salsa

Servings: 6
Cooking Time: 16 Minutes

Ingredients:
- 4 cups (one 1-pound eggplant) Purple Italian eggplant(s), stemmed and diced (no need to peel)
- Olive oil spray
- 1½ cups Celery, thinly sliced
- 16 (about ½ pound) Cherry or grape tomatoes, halved
- 1 tablespoon Drained and rinsed capers, chopped
- Up to 1 tablespoon Minced fresh rosemary leaves
- 1½ tablespoons Red wine vinegar
- 1½ teaspoons Granulated white sugar
- ¾ teaspoon Table salt
- ¾ teaspoon Ground black pepper

Directions:
1. Preheat the air fryer to 350°F .
2. Put the eggplant pieces in a bowl and generously coat them with olive oil spray. Toss and stir, spray again, and toss some more, until the pieces are glistening.
3. When the machine is at temperature, pour the eggplant pieces into the basket and spread them out into an even layer. Air-fry for 8 minutes, tossing and rearranging the pieces twice.

4. Meanwhile, put the celery and tomatoes in the same bowl the eggplant pieces had been in. Generously coat them with olive oil spray; then toss well, spray again, and toss some more, until the vegetables are well coated.

5. When the eggplant has cooked for 8 minutes, pour the celery and tomatoes on top in the basket. Air-fry undisturbed for 8 minutes more, until the tomatoes have begun to soften.

6. Pour the contents of the basket back into the same bowl. Add the capers, rosemary, vinegar, sugar, salt, and pepper. Toss well to blend, breaking up the tomatoes a bit to create more moisture in the mixture.

7. Cover and refrigerate for 2 hours to blend the flavors. Serve chilled or at room temperature. The caponata salsa can stay in its covered bowl in the fridge for up to 2 days before the vegetables weep too much moisture and the dish becomes too wet.

Bagel Chips

Servings: 2
Cooking Time: 4 Minutes

Ingredients:
- Sweet
- 1 large plain bagel
- 2 teaspoons sugar
- 1 teaspoon ground cinnamon
- butter-flavored cooking spray
- Savory
- 1 large plain bagel
- 1 teaspoon Italian seasoning
- ½ teaspoon garlic powder
- oil for misting or cooking spray

Directions:
1. Preheat air fryer to 390°F.
2. Cut bagel into ¼-inch slices or thinner.

3. Mix the seasonings together.

4. Spread out the slices, mist with oil or cooking spray, and sprinkle with half of the seasonings.

5. Turn over and repeat to coat the other side with oil or cooking spray and seasonings.

6. Place in air fryer basket and cook for 2minutes. Shake basket or stir a little and continue cooking for 2 minutes or until toasty brown and crispy.

Potato Chips

Servings: 2
Cooking Time: 15 Minutes

Ingredients:

- 2 medium potatoes
- 2 teaspoons extra-light olive oil
- oil for misting or cooking spray
- salt and pepper

Directions:

1. Peel the potatoes.

2. Using a mandoline or paring knife, shave potatoes into thin slices, dropping them into a bowl of water as you cut them.

3. Dry potatoes as thoroughly as possible with paper towels or a clean dish towel. Toss potato slices with the oil to coat completely.

4. Spray air fryer basket with cooking spray and add potato slices.

5. Stir and separate with a fork.

6. Cook 390°F for 5minutes. Stir and separate potato slices. Cook 5 more minutes. Stir and separate potatoes again. Cook another 5minutes.

7. Season to taste.

Blistered Shishito Peppers

Servings: 3
Cooking Time: 5 Minutes

Ingredients:

- 6 ounces (about 18) Shishito peppers
- Vegetable oil spray
- For garnishing Coarse sea or kosher salt and lemon wedges

Directions:

1. Preheat the air fryer to 400°F.

2. Put the peppers in a bowl and lightly coat them with vegetable oil spray. Toss gently, spray again, and toss until the peppers are glistening but not drenched.

3. Pour the peppers into the basket, spread them into as close to one layer as you can, and air-fry for 5 minutes, tossing and rearranging the peppers at the 2- and 4-minute marks, until the peppers are blistered and even blackened in spots.

4. Pour the peppers into a bowl, add salt to taste, and toss gently. Serve the peppers with lemon wedges to squeeze over them.

Crunchy Spicy Chickpeas

Servings: 6
Cooking Time: 12 Minutes

Ingredients:

- 2½ cups Canned chickpeas, drained and rinsed
- 2½ tablespoons Vegetable or canola oil
- up to 1 tablespoon Cajun or jerk dried seasoning blend (see here for a Cajun blend, here for a jerk blend)
- up to ¾ teaspoon Table salt (optional)

Directions:

1. Preheat the air fryer to 400°F.

2. Toss the chickpeas, oil, seasoning blend, and salt (if using) in a large bowl until the chickpeas are evenly coated.

3. When the machine is at temperature, pour the chickpeas into the basket. Air-fry for 12 minutes, removing the basket at the 4- and 8-minute marks to toss and rearrange the chickpeas, until very aromatic and perhaps sizzling but not burned.

4. Pour the chickpeas into a large serving bowl. Cool for a couple of minutes, gently stirring once, before you dive in.

Cheese Arancini

Servings: 8
Cooking Time: 12 Minutes

Ingredients:
- 1 cup Water
- ½ cup Raw white Arborio rice
- 1½ teaspoons Butter
- ¼ teaspoon Table salt
- 8 ¾-inch semi-firm mozzarella cubes (not fresh mozzarella)
- 2 Large egg(s), well beaten
- 1 cup Seasoned Italian-style dried bread crumbs (gluten-free, if a concern)
- Olive oil spray

Directions:
1. Combine the water, rice, butter, and salt in a small saucepan. Bring to a boil over medium-high heat, stirring occasionally. Cover, reduce the heat to very low, and simmer very slowly for 20 minutes.

2. Take the saucepan off the heat and let it stand, covered, for 10 minutes. Uncover it and fluff the rice. Cool for 20 minutes. (The rice can be made up to 1 hour in advance; keep it covered in its saucepan.)

3. Preheat the air fryer to 375°F .

4. Set up and fill two shallow soup plates or small bowls on your counter: one with the beaten egg(s) and one with the bread crumbs.

5. With clean but wet hands, scoop up about 2 tablespoons of the cooked rice and form it into a ball. Push a cube of mozzarella into the middle of the ball and seal the cheese inside. Dip the ball in the egg(s) to coat completely, letting any excess egg slip back into the rest. Roll the ball in the bread crumbs to coat evenly but lightly. Set aside and continue making more rice balls.

6. Generously spray the balls with olive oil spray, then set them in the basket in one layer. They must not touch. Air-fry undisturbed for 10 minutes, or until crunchy and golden brown. If the machine is at 360°F, you may need to add 2 minutes to the cooking time.

7. Use a nonstick-safe spatula, and maybe a flatware spoon for balance, to gently transfer the balls to a wire rack. Cool for at least 5 minutes or up to 20 minutes before serving.

Sweet-and-salty Pretzels

Servings: 4
Cooking Time: 5 Minutes

Ingredients:
- 2 cups Plain pretzel nuggets
- 1 tablespoon Worcestershire sauce
- 2 teaspoons Granulated white sugar
- 1 teaspoon Mild smoked paprika
- ½ teaspoon Garlic or onion powder

Directions:
1. Preheat the air fryer to 350°F .

2. Put the pretzel nuggets, Worcestershire sauce, sugar, smoked paprika, and garlic or onion powder in a large bowl. Toss gently until the nuggets are well coated.

3. When the machine is at temperature, pour the nuggets into the basket, spreading them into as close to a single layer as possible. Air-fry, shaking the basket three or four times to rearrange the nuggets, for 5 minutes, or until the nuggets are toasted and aromatic. Although the coating will darken, don't let it burn, especially if the machine's temperature is 360°F.

4. Pour the nuggets onto a wire rack and gently spread them into one layer. (A rubber spatula does a good job.) Cool for 5 minutes before serving.

Corn Dog Bites

Servings: 3

Cooking Time: 12 Minutes

Ingredients:

- 3 cups Purchased cornbread stuffing mix
- ⅓ cup All-purpose flour
- 2 Large egg(s), well beaten
- 3 Hot dogs, cut into 2-inch pieces (vegetarian hot dogs, if preferred)
- Vegetable oil spray

Directions:

1. Preheat the air fryer to 375°F .

2. Put the cornbread stuffing mix in a food processor. Cover and pulse to grind into a mixture like fine bread crumbs.

3. Set up and fill three shallow soup plates or small pie plates on your counter: one for the flour, one for the egg(s), and one for the stuffing mix crumbs.

4. Dip a hot dog piece in the flour to coat it completely, then gently shake off any excess. Dip the hot dog piece into the egg(s) and gently roll it around to coat all surfaces, then pick it up and allow any excess egg to slip back into the rest. Set the hot dog piece in the stuffing mix crumbs and roll it gently to coat it evenly and well on all sides, even the ends. Set it aside on a cutting board and continue dipping and coating the remaining hot dog pieces.

5. Give the coated hot dog pieces a generous coating of vegetable oil spray on all sides, then set them in the basket in one layer with some space between them. Air-fry undisturbed for 10 minutes, or until golden brown and crunchy. (You'll need to add 2 minutes in the air fryer if the temperature is at 360°F.)

6. Use a nonstick-safe spatula, and perhaps a flatware fork for balance, to transfer the corn dog bites to a wire rack. Cool for 5 minutes before serving.

Spicy Chicken And Pepper Jack Cheese Bites

Servings: 8

Cooking Time: 8 Minutes

Ingredients:

- 8 ounces cream cheese, softened
- 2 cups grated pepper jack cheese
- 1 Jalapeño pepper, diced
- 2 scallions, minced
- 1 teaspoon paprika
- 2 teaspoons salt, divided
- 3 cups shredded cooked chicken
- ¼ cup all-purpose flour*
- 2 eggs, lightly beaten
- 1 cup panko breadcrumbs*
- olive oil, in a spray bottle
- salsa

Directions:

1. Beat the cream cheese in a bowl until it is smooth and easy to stir. Add the pepper jack

cheese, Jalapeño pepper, scallions, paprika and 1 teaspoon of salt. Fold in the shredded cooked chicken and combine well. Roll this mixture into 1-inch balls.

2. Set up a dredging station with three shallow dishes. Place the flour into one shallow dish. Place the eggs into a second shallow dish. Finally, combine the panko breadcrumbs and remaining teaspoon of salt in a third dish.

3. Coat the chicken cheese balls by rolling each ball in the flour first, then dip them into the eggs and finally roll them in the panko breadcrumbs to coat all sides. Refrigerate for at least 30 minutes.

4. Preheat the air fryer to 400°F.

5. Spray the chicken cheese balls with oil and air-fry in batches for 8 minutes. Shake the basket a few times throughout the cooking process to help the balls brown evenly.

6. Serve hot with salsa on the side.

VEGETABLE SIDE DISHES RECIPES

Mashed Sweet Potato Tots

Servings: 18
Cooking Time: 12 Minutes

Ingredients:

* 1 cup cooked mashed sweet potatoes
* 1 egg white, beaten
* ⅛ teaspoon ground cinnamon
* 1 dash nutmeg
* 2 tablespoons chopped pecans
* 1½ teaspoons honey
* salt
* ½ cup panko breadcrumbs
* oil for misting or cooking spray

Directions:

1. Preheat air fryer to 390°F.
2. In a large bowl, mix together the potatoes, egg white, cinnamon, nutmeg, pecans, honey, and salt to taste.
3. Place panko crumbs on a sheet of wax paper.
4. For each tot, use about 2 teaspoons of sweet potato mixture. To shape, drop the measure of potato mixture onto panko crumbs and push crumbs up and around potatoes to coat edges. Then turn tot over to coat other side with crumbs.
5. Mist tots with oil or cooking spray and place in air fryer basket in single layer.
6. Cook at 390°F for 12 minutes, until browned and crispy.
7. Repeat steps 5 and 6 to cook remaining tots.

Roasted Brussels Sprouts

Servings: 4
Cooking Time: 25 Minutes

Ingredients:

* ½ cup balsamic vinegar
* 2 tablespoons honey
* 1 pound Brussels sprouts, halved lengthwise
* 2 slices bacon, chopped
* ½ teaspoon garlic powder
* 1 teaspoon salt
* 1 tablespoon extra-virgin olive oil
* ¼ cup grated Parmesan cheese

Directions:

1. Preheat the air fryer to 370°F.
2. In a small saucepan, heat the vinegar and honey for 8 to 10 minutes over medium-low heat, or until the balsamic vinegar reduces by half to create a thick balsamic glazing sauce.
3. While the balsamic glaze is reducing, in a large bowl, toss together the Brussels sprouts, bacon, garlic powder, salt, and olive oil. Pour the mixture into the air fryer basket and cook for 10 minutes; check for doneness. Cook another 2 to 5 minutes or until slightly crispy and tender.
4. Pour the balsamic glaze into a serving bowl and add the cooked Brussels sprouts to the dish, stirring to coat. Top with grated Parmesan cheese and serve.

Buttery Stuffed Tomatoes

Servings: 6
Cooking Time: 15 Minutes

Ingredients:

* 3 8-ounce round tomatoes
* ½ cup plus 1 tablespoon Plain panko bread crumbs (gluten-free, if a concern)
* 3 tablespoons (about ½ ounce) Finely grated Parmesan cheese

- 3 tablespoons Butter, melted and cooled
- 4 teaspoons Stemmed and chopped fresh parsley leaves
- 1 teaspoon Minced garlic
- ¼ teaspoon Table salt
- Up to ¼ teaspoon Red pepper flakes
- Olive oil spray

Directions:

1. Preheat the air fryer to 375°F .
2. Cut the tomatoes in half through their "equators" (that is, not through the stem ends). One at a time, gently squeeze the tomato halves over a trash can, using a clean finger to gently force out the seeds and most of the juice inside, working carefully so that the tomato doesn't lose its round shape or get crushed.
3. Stir the bread crumbs, cheese, butter, parsley, garlic, salt, and red pepper flakes in a bowl until the bread crumbs are moistened and the parsley is uniform throughout the mixture. Pile this mixture into the spaces left in the tomato halves. Press gently to compact the filling. Coat the tops of the tomatoes with olive oil spray.
4. Place the tomatoes cut side up in the basket. They may touch each other. Air-fry for 15 minutes, or until the filling is lightly browned and crunchy.
5. Use nonstick-safe spatula and kitchen tongs for balance to gently transfer the stuffed tomatoes to a platter or a cutting board. Cool for a couple of minutes before serving.

Green Beans

Servings: 4
Cooking Time: 12 Minutes

Ingredients:

- 1 pound fresh green beans
- 2 tablespoons Italian salad dressing
- salt and pepper

Directions:

1. Wash beans and snap off stem ends.
2. In a large bowl, toss beans with Italian dressing.
3. Cook at 330°F for 5minutes. Shake basket or stir and cook 5minutes longer. Shake basket again and, if needed, continue cooking for 2 minutes, until as tender as you like. Beans should shrivel slightly and brown in places.
4. Sprinkle with salt and pepper to taste.

Zucchini Boats With Ham And Cheese

Servings: 4
Cooking Time: 12 Minutes

Ingredients:

- 2 6-inch-long zucchini
- 2 ounces Thinly sliced deli ham, any rind removed, meat roughly chopped
- 4 Dry-packed sun-dried tomatoes, chopped
- ⅓ cup Purchased pesto
- ¼ cup Packaged mini croutons
- ¼ cup (about 1 ounce) Shredded semi-firm mozzarella cheese

Directions:

1. Preheat the air fryer to 375°F .
2. Split the zucchini in half lengthwise and use a flatware spoon or a serrated grapefruit spoon to scoop out the insides of the halves, leaving at least a ¼-inch border all around the zucchini half. (You can save the scooped out insides to add to soups and stews—or even freeze it for a much later use.)

3. Mix the ham, sun-dried tomatoes, pesto, croutons, and half the cheese in a bowl until well combined. Pack this mixture into the zucchini "shells." Top them with the remaining cheese.

4. Set them stuffing side up in the basket without touching (even a fraction of an inch between them is enough room). Air-fry undisturbed for 12 minutes, or until softened and browned, with the cheese melted on top.

5. Use a nonstick-safe spatula to transfer the zucchini boats stuffing side up on a wire rack. Cool for 5 or 10 minutes before serving.

Steamboat Shrimp Salad

Servings: 4

Cooking Time: 4 Minutes

Ingredients:

- Steamboat Dressing
- ½ cup mayonnaise
- ½ cup plain yogurt
- 2 teaspoons freshly squeezed lemon juice (no substitutes)
- 2 teaspoons grated lemon rind
- 1 teaspoon dill weed, slightly crushed
- ½ teaspoon hot sauce
- Steamed Shrimp
- 24 small, raw shrimp, peeled and deveined
- 1 teaspoon lemon juice
- ¼ teaspoon Old Bay Seasoning
- Salad
- 8 cups romaine or Bibb lettuce, chopped or torn
- ¼ cup red onion, cut in thin slivers
- 12 black olives, sliced
- 12 cherry or grape tomatoes, halved
- 1 medium avocado, sliced or cut into large chunks

Directions:

1. Combine all dressing ingredients and mix well. Refrigerate while preparing shrimp and salad.

2. Sprinkle raw shrimp with lemon juice and Old Bay Seasoning. Use more Old Bay if you like your shrimp bold and spicy.

3. Pour 4 tablespoons of water in bottom of air fryer.

4. Place shrimp in air fryer basket in single layer.

5. Cook at 390°F for 4 minutes. Remove shrimp from basket and place in refrigerator to cool.

6. Combine all salad ingredients and mix gently. Divide among 4 salad plates or bowls.

7. Top each salad with 6 shrimp and serve with dressing.

Stuffed Onions

Servings: 6

Cooking Time: 27 Minutes

Ingredients:

- 6 Small 3½- to 4-ounce yellow or white onions
- Olive oil spray
- 6 ounces Bulk sweet Italian sausage meat (gluten-free, if a concern)
- 9 Cherry tomatoes, chopped
- 3 tablespoons Seasoned Italian-style dried bread crumbs (gluten-free, if a concern)
- 3 tablespoons (about ½ ounce) Finely grated Parmesan cheese

Directions:

1. Preheat the air fryer to 325°F (or 330°F, if that's the closest setting).

2. Cut just enough off the root ends of the onions so they will stand up on a cutting board when this end is turned down. Carefully peel off just the brown, papery skin. Now cut the top

quarter off each and place the onion back on the cutting board with this end facing up. Use a flatware spoon (preferably a serrated grapefruit spoon) or a melon baller to scoop out the "insides" (interior layers) of the onion, leaving enough of the bottom and side walls so that the onion does not collapse. Depending on the thickness of the layers in the onion, this may be one or two of those layers—or even three, if they're very thin.

3. Coat the insides and outsides of the onions with olive oil spray. Set the onion "shells" in the basket and air-fry for 15 minutes.

4. Meanwhile, make the filling. Set a medium skillet over medium heat for a couple of minutes, then crumble in the sausage meat. Cook, stirring often, until browned, about 4 minutes. Transfer the contents of the skillet to a medium bowl (leave the fat behind in the skillet or add it to the bowl, depending on your cross-trainer regimen). Stir in the tomatoes, bread crumbs, and cheese until well combined.

5. When the onions are ready, use a nonstick-safe spatula to gently transfer them to a cutting board. Increase the air fryer's temperature to 350°F .

6. Pack the sausage mixture into the onion shells, gently compacting the filling and mounding it up at the top.

7. When the machine is at temperature, set the onions stuffing side up in the basket with at least ¼ inch between them. Air-fry for 12 minutes, or until lightly browned and sizzling hot.

8. Use a nonstick-safe spatula, and perhaps a flatware fork for balance, to transfer the onions to a cutting board or serving platter. Cool for 5 minutes before serving.

Tandoori Cauliflower

Servings: 4
Cooking Time: 10 Minutes

Ingredients:
- ½ cup Plain full-fat yogurt (not Greek yogurt)
- 1½ teaspoons Yellow curry powder, purchased or homemade (see the headnote)
- 1½ teaspoons Lemon juice
- ¾ teaspoon Table salt (optional)
- 4½ cups (about 1 pound 2 ounces) 2-inch cauliflower florets

Directions:
1. Preheat the air fryer to 400°F.
2. Whisk the yogurt, curry powder, lemon juice, and salt (if using) in a large bowl until uniform. Add the florets and stir gently to coat the florets well and evenly. Even better, use your clean, dry hands to get the yogurt mixture down into all the nooks of the florets.
3. When the machine is at temperature, transfer the florets to the basket, spreading them gently into as close to one layer as you can. Air-fry for 10 minutes, tossing and rearranging the florets twice so that any covered or touching parts are exposed to the air currents, until lightly browned and tender if still a bit crunchy.
4. Pour the contents of the basket onto a wire rack. Cool for at least 5 minutes before serving, or serve at room temperature.

French Fries

Servings: 4
Cooking Time: 25 Minutes

Ingredients:

- 2 cups fresh potatoes
- 2 teaspoons oil
- ½ teaspoon salt

Directions:

1. Cut potatoes into ½-inch-wide slices, then lay slices flat and cut into ½-inch sticks.
2. Rinse potato sticks and blot dry with a clean towel.
3. In a bowl or sealable plastic bag, mix the potatoes, oil, and salt together.
4. Pour into air fryer basket.
5. Cook at 390°F for 10minutes. Shake basket to redistribute fries and continue cooking for approximately 15minutes, until fries are golden brown.

Blistered Green Beans

Servings: 3
Cooking Time: 10 Minutes

Ingredients:

- ¾ pound Green beans, trimmed on both ends
- 1½ tablespoons Olive oil
- 3 tablespoons Pine nuts
- 1½ tablespoons Balsamic vinegar
- 1½ teaspoons Minced garlic
- ¾ teaspoon Table salt
- ¾ teaspoon Ground black pepper

Directions:

1. Preheat the air fryer to 400°F.
2. Toss the green beans and oil in a large bowl until all the green beans are glistening.
3. When the machine is at temperature, pile the green beans into the basket. Air-fry for 10 minutes, tossing often to rearrange the green beans in the basket, or until blistered and tender.
4. Dump the contents of the basket into a serving bowl. Add the pine nuts, vinegar, garlic, salt, and pepper. Toss well to coat and combine. Serve warm or at room temperature.

Green Peas With Mint

Servings: 4
Cooking Time: 5 Minutes

Ingredients:

- 1 cup shredded lettuce
- 1 10-ounce package frozen green peas, thawed
- 1 tablespoon fresh mint, shredded
- 1 teaspoon melted butter

Directions:

1. Lay the shredded lettuce in the air fryer basket.
2. Toss together the peas, mint, and melted butter and spoon over the lettuce.
3. Cook at 360°F for 5minutes, until peas are warm and lettuce wilts.

Grits Again

Servings: 2
Cooking Time: 10 Minutes

Ingredients:

- cooked grits
- plain breadcrumbs
- oil for misting or cooking spray
- honey or maple syrup for serving (optional)

Directions:

1. While grits are still warm, spread them into a square or rectangular baking pan, about ½-inch thick. If your grits are thicker than that, scoop some out into another pan.

2. Chill several hours or overnight, until grits are cold and firm.

3. When ready to cook, pour off any water that has collected in pan and cut grits into 2- to 3-inch squares.

4. Dip grits squares in breadcrumbs and place in air fryer basket in single layer, close but not touching.

5. Cook at 390°F for 10 minutes, until heated through and crispy brown on the outside.

6. Serve while hot either plain or with a drizzle of honey or maple syrup.

Broccoli Tots

Servings: 24
Cooking Time: 10 Minutes

Ingredients:

- 2 cups broccoli florets (about ½ pound broccoli crowns)
- 1 egg, beaten
- ⅛ teaspoon onion powder
- ¼ teaspoon salt
- ⅛ teaspoon pepper
- 2 tablespoons grated Parmesan cheese
- ¼ cup panko breadcrumbs
- oil for misting

Directions:

1. Steam broccoli for 2minutes. Rinse in cold water, drain well, and chop finely.

2. In a large bowl, mix broccoli with all other ingredients except the oil.

3. Scoop out small portions of mixture and shape into 24 tots. Lay them on a cookie sheet or wax paper as you work.

4. Spray tots with oil and place in air fryer basket in single layer.

5. Cook at 390°F for 5minutes. Shake basket and spray with oil again. Cook 5minutes longer or until browned and crispy.

Parmesan Asparagus

Servings: 2
Cooking Time: 5 Minutes

Ingredients:

- 1 bunch asparagus, stems trimmed
- 1 teaspoon olive oil
- salt and freshly ground black pepper
- ¼ cup coarsely grated Parmesan cheese
- ½ lemon

Directions:

1. Preheat the air fryer to 400°F.

2. Toss the asparagus with the oil and season with salt and freshly ground black pepper.

3. Transfer the asparagus to the air fryer basket and air-fry at 400°F for 5 minutes, shaking the basket to turn the asparagus once or twice during the cooking process.

4. When the asparagus is cooked to your liking, sprinkle the asparagus generously with the Parmesan cheese and close the air fryer drawer again. Let the asparagus sit for 1 minute in the turned-off air fryer. Then, remove the asparagus, transfer it to a serving dish and finish with a grind of black pepper and a squeeze of lemon juice.

Shoestring Butternut Squash Fries

Servings: 3
Cooking Time: 16 Minutes

Ingredients:
- 1 pound 2 ounces Spiralized butternut squash strands
- Vegetable oil spray
- To taste Coarse sea salt or kosher salt

Directions:
1. Preheat the air fryer to 375°F .
2. Place the spiralized squash in a big bowl. Coat the strands with vegetable oil spray, toss well, coat again, and toss several times to make sure all the strands have been oiled.
3. When the machine is at temperature, pour the strands into the basket and spread them out into as even a layer as possible. Air-fry for 16 minutes, tossing and rearranging the strands every 4 minutes, or until they're lightly browned and crisp.
4. Pour the contents of the basket into a serving bowl, add salt to taste, and toss well before serving hot.

Chicken Eggrolls

Servings: 10
Cooking Time: 17 Minutes

Ingredients:
- 1 tablespoon vegetable oil
- ¼ cup chopped onion
- 1 clove garlic, minced
- 1 cup shredded carrot
- ½ cup thinly sliced celery
- 2 cups cooked chicken
- 2 cups shredded white cabbage
- ½ cup teriyaki sauce
- 20 egg roll wrappers
- 1 egg, whisked
- 1 tablespoon water

Directions:
1. Preheat the air fryer to 390°F.
2. In a large skillet, heat the oil over medium-high heat. Add in the onion and sauté for 1 minute. Add in the garlic and sauté for 30 seconds. Add in the carrot and celery and cook for 2 minutes. Add in the chicken, cabbage, and teriyaki sauce. Allow the mixture to cook for 1 minute, stirring to combine. Remove from the heat.
3. In a small bowl, whisk together the egg and water for brushing the edges.
4. Lay the eggroll wrappers out at an angle. Place ¼ cup filling in the center. Fold the bottom corner up first and then fold in the corners; roll up to complete eggroll.
5. Place the eggrolls in the air fryer basket, spray with cooking spray, and cook for 8 minutes, turn over, and cook another 2 to 4 minutes.

Moroccan Cauliflower

Servings: 6
Cooking Time: 15 Minutes

Ingredients:
- 1 tablespoon curry powder
- 2 teaspoons smoky paprika
- ½ teaspoon ground cumin
- ½ teaspoon salt
- 1 head cauliflower, cut into bite-size pieces
- ¼ cup red wine vinegar
- 2 tablespoons extra-virgin olive oil
- 2 tablespoons chopped parsley

Directions:

1. Preheat the air fryer to 370°F.

2. In a large bowl, mix the curry powder, paprika, cumin, and salt. Add the cauliflower and stir to coat. Pour the red wine vinegar over the top and continue stirring.

3. Place the cauliflower into the air fryer basket; drizzle olive oil over the top.

4. Cook the cauliflower for 5 minutes, toss, and cook another 5 minutes. Raise the temperature to 400°F and continue cooking for 4 to 6 minutes, or until crispy.

Sesame Carrots And Sugar Snap Peas

Servings: 4
Cooking Time: 16 Minutes

Ingredients:

- 1 pound carrots, peeled sliced on the bias (½-inch slices)
- 1 teaspoon olive oil
- salt and freshly ground black pepper
- ⅓ cup honey
- 1 tablespoon sesame oil
- 1 tablespoon soy sauce
- ½ teaspoon minced fresh ginger
- 4 ounces sugar snap peas (about 1 cup)
- 1½ teaspoons sesame seeds

Directions:

1. Preheat the air fryer to 360°F.

2. Toss the carrots with the olive oil, season with salt and pepper and air-fry for 10 minutes, shaking the basket once or twice during the cooking process.

3. Combine the honey, sesame oil, soy sauce and minced ginger in a large bowl. Add the sugar snap peas and the air-fried carrots to the honey mixture, toss to coat and return everything to the air fryer basket.

4. Turn up the temperature to 400°F and air-fry for an additional 6 minutes, shaking the basket once during the cooking process.

5. Transfer the carrots and sugar snap peas to a serving bowl. Pour the sauce from the bottom of the cooker over the vegetables and sprinkle sesame seeds over top. Serve immediately.

Mashed Potato Pancakes

Servings: 6
Cooking Time: 10 Minutes

Ingredients:

- 2 cups leftover mashed potatoes
- ½ cup grated cheddar cheese
- ¼ cup thinly sliced green onions
- ½ teaspoon salt
- ¼ teaspoon black pepper
- 1 cup breadcrumbs

Directions:

1. Preheat the air fryer to 380°F.

2. In a large bowl, mix together the potatoes, cheese, and onions. Using a ¼ cup measuring cup, measure out 6 patties. Form the potatoes into ½-inch thick patties. Season the patties with salt and pepper on both sides.

3. In a small bowl, place the breadcrumbs. Gently press the potato pancakes into the breadcrumbs.

4. Place the potato pancakes into the air fryer basket and spray with cooking spray. Cook for 5 minutes, turn the pancakes over, and cook another 3 to 5 minutes or until golden brown on the outside and cooked through on the inside.

Roasted Garlic And Thyme Tomatoes

Servings: 2
Cooking Time: 15 Minutes

Ingredients:
- 4 Roma tomatoes
- 1 tablespoon olive oil
- salt and freshly ground black pepper
- 1 clove garlic, minced
- ½ teaspoon dried thyme

Directions:
1. Preheat the air fryer to 390°F.
2. Cut the tomatoes in half and scoop out the seeds and any pithy parts with your fingers. Place the tomatoes in a bowl and toss with the olive oil, salt, pepper, garlic and thyme.
3. Transfer the tomatoes to the air fryer, cut side up. Air-fry for 15 minutes. The edges should just start to brown. Let the tomatoes cool to an edible temperature for a few minutes and then use in pastas, on top of crostini, or as an accompaniment to any poultry, meat or fish.

Zucchini Fries

Servings: 3
Cooking Time: 12 Minutes

Ingredients:
- 1 large Zucchini
- ½ cup All-purpose flour or tapioca flour
- 2 Large egg(s), well beaten
- 1 cup Seasoned Italian-style dried bread crumbs (gluten-free, if a concern)
- Olive oil spray

Directions:
1. Preheat the air fryer to 400°F.
2. Trim the zucchini into a long rectangular block, taking off the ends and four "sides" to make this shape. Cut the block lengthwise into ½-inch-thick slices. Lay these slices flat and cut in half widthwise. Slice each of these pieces into ½-inch-thick batons.
3. Set up and fill three shallow soup plates or small pie plates on your counter: one for the flour, one for the beaten egg(s), and one for the bread crumbs.
4. Set a zucchini baton in the flour and turn it several times to coat all sides. Gently shake off any excess flour, then dip it in the egg(s), turning it to coat. Let any excess egg slip back into the rest, then set the baton in the bread crumbs and turn it several times, pressing gently to coat all sides, even the ends. Set aside on a cutting board and continue coating the remainder of the batons in the same way.
5. Lightly coat the batons on all sides with olive oil spray. Set them in two flat layers in the basket, the top layer at a 90-degree angle to the bottom one, with a little air space between the batons in each layer. In the end, the whole thing will look like a crosshatch pattern. Air-fry undisturbed for 6 minutes.
6. Use kitchen tongs to gently rearrange the batons so that any covered parts are now uncovered. The batons no longer need to be in a crosshatch pattern. Continue air-frying undisturbed for 6 minutes, or until lightly browned and crisp.
7. Gently pour the contents of the basket onto a wire rack. Spread the batons out and cool for only a minute or two before serving.

Five-spice Roasted Sweet Potatoes

Servings: 4

Cooking Time: 12 Minutes

Ingredients:

- ½ teaspoon ground cinnamon
- ¼ teaspoon ground cumin
- ¼ teaspoon paprika
- 1 teaspoon chile powder
- ⅛ teaspoon turmeric
- ½ teaspoon salt (optional)
- freshly ground black pepper
- 2 large sweet potatoes, peeled and cut into ¾-inch cubes (about 3 cups)
- 1 tablespoon olive oil

Directions:

1. In a large bowl, mix together cinnamon, cumin, paprika, chile powder, turmeric, salt, and pepper to taste.

2. Add potatoes and stir well.

3. Drizzle the seasoned potatoes with the olive oil and stir until evenly coated.

4. Place seasoned potatoes in the air fryer baking pan or an ovenproof dish that fits inside your air fryer basket.

5. Cook for 6minutes at 390°F, stop, and stir well.

6. Cook for an additional 6minutes.

Hasselback Garlic-and-butter Potatoes

Servings: 3

Cooking Time: 48 Minutes

Ingredients:

- 3 8-ounce russet potatoes
- 6 Brown button or Baby Bella mushrooms, very thinly sliced
- Olive oil spray
- 3 tablespoons Butter, melted and cooled
- 1 tablespoon Minced garlic
- ¾ teaspoon Table salt
- 3 tablespoons (about ½ ounce) Finely grated Parmesan cheese

Directions:

1. Preheat the air fryer to 350°F .

2. Cut slits down the length of each potato, about three-quarters down into the potato and spaced about ¼ inch apart. Wedge a thin mushroom slice in each slit. Generously coat the potatoes on all sides with olive oil spray.

3. When the machine is at temperature, set the potatoes mushroom side up in the basket with as much air space between them as possible. Air-fry undisturbed for 45 minutes, or tender when pricked with a fork.

4. Increase the machine's temperature to 400°F. Use kitchen tongs, and perhaps a flatware fork for balance, to gently transfer the potatoes to a cutting board. Brush each evenly with butter, then sprinkle the minced garlic and salt over them. Sprinkle the cheese evenly over the potatoes.

5. Use those same tongs to gently transfer the potatoes cheese side up to the basket in one layer with some space for air flow between them. Air-fry undisturbed for 3 minutes, or until the cheese has melted and begun to brown.

6. Use those same tongs to gently transfer the potatoes back to the wire rack. Cool for 5 minutes before serving.

Polenta

Servings: 4

Cooking Time: 15 Minutes

Ingredients:

- 1 pound polenta
- ¼ cup flour
- oil for misting or cooking spray

Directions:

1. Cut polenta into ½-inch slices.

2. Dip slices in flour to coat well. Spray both sides with oil or cooking spray.

3. Cook at 390°F for 5minutes. Turn polenta and spray both sides again with oil.

4. Cook 10 more minutes or until brown and crispy.

Roasted Ratatouille Vegetables

Servings: 2

Cooking Time: 15 Minutes

Ingredients:

- 1 baby or Japanese eggplant, cut into 1½-inch cubes
- 1 red pepper, cut into 1-inch chunks
- 1 yellow pepper, cut into 1-inch chunks
- 1 zucchini, cut into 1-inch chunks
- 1 clove garlic, minced
- ½ teaspoon dried basil
- 1 tablespoon olive oil
- salt and freshly ground black pepper
- ¼ cup sliced sun-dried tomatoes in oil
- 2 tablespoons chopped fresh basil

Directions:

1. Preheat the air fryer to 400°F.

2. Toss the eggplant, peppers and zucchini with the garlic, dried basil, olive oil, salt and freshly ground black pepper.

3. Air-fry the vegetables at 400°F for 15 minutes, shaking the basket a few times during the cooking process to redistribute the ingredients.

4. As soon as the vegetables are tender, toss them with the sliced sun-dried tomatoes and fresh basil and serve.

BREAD AND BREAKFAST

French Toast Sticks

Servings: 4
Cooking Time: 7 Minutes

Ingredients:

- 2 eggs
- ½ cup milk
- ⅛ teaspoon salt
- ½ teaspoon pure vanilla extract
- ¾ cup crushed cornflakes
- 6 slices sandwich bread, each slice cut into 4 strips
- oil for misting or cooking spray
- maple syrup or honey

Directions:

1. In a small bowl, beat together eggs, milk, salt, and vanilla.
2. Place crushed cornflakes on a plate or in a shallow dish.
3. Dip bread strips in egg mixture, shake off excess, and roll in cornflake crumbs.
4. Spray both sides of bread strips with oil.
5. Place bread strips in air fryer basket in single layer.
6. Cook at 390°F for 7minutes or until they're dark golden brown.
7. Repeat steps 5 and 6 to cook remaining French toast sticks.
8. Serve with maple syrup or honey for dipping.

Baked Eggs

Servings: 4
Cooking Time: 6 Minutes

Ingredients:

- 4 large eggs
- ⅛ teaspoon black pepper
- ⅛ teaspoon salt

Directions:

1. Preheat the air fryer to 330°F. Place 4 silicone muffin liners into the air fryer basket.
2. Crack 1 egg at a time into each silicone muffin liner. Sprinkle with black pepper and salt.
3. Bake for 6 minutes. Remove and let cool 2 minutes prior to serving.

Sweet And Spicy Pumpkin Scones

Servings: 8
Cooking Time: 8 Minutes

Ingredients:

- 2 cups all-purpose flour
- 3 tablespoons packed brown sugar
- ½ teaspoon baking powder
- ¼ teaspoon baking soda
- ½ teaspoon kosher salt
- ½ teaspoon ground cinnamon
- ¼ teaspoon ground ginger
- ¼ teaspoon ground cardamom
- 4 tablespoons cold unsalted butter
- ½ cup plus 2 tablespoons pumpkin puree, divided
- 4 tablespoons milk, divided
- 1 large egg
- 1 cup powdered sugar

Directions:

1. In a large bowl, mix together the flour, brown sugar, baking powder, baking soda, salt, cinnamon, ginger, and cardamom. Using a pastry blender or two knives, cut in the butter until coarse crumbles appear.

2. In a small bowl, whisk together ½ cup of the pumpkin puree, 2 tablespoons of the milk, and the egg until combined. Pour the wet ingredients into the dry ingredients; stir to combine.

3. Form the dough into a ball and place onto a floured service. Press the dough out or use a rolling pin to roll out the dough until ½ inch thick and in a circle. Cut the dough into 8 wedges.

4. Bake at 360°F for 8 to 10 minutes or until completely cooked through. Cook in batches as needed.

5. In a medium bowl, whisk together the powdered sugar, the remaining 2 tablespoons of pumpkin puree, and the remaining 2 tablespoons of milk. When the pumpkin scones have cooled, drizzle the pumpkin glaze over the top before serving.

Pumpkin Loaf

Servings: 6
Cooking Time: 22 Minutes

Ingredients:

- cooking spray
- 1 large egg
- ½ cup granulated sugar
- ⅓ cup oil
- ½ cup canned pumpkin (not pie filling)
- ½ teaspoon vanilla
- ⅔ cup flour plus 1 tablespoon
- ½ teaspoon baking powder
- ½ teaspoon baking soda
- ½ teaspoon salt
- 1 teaspoon pumpkin pie spice
- ¼ teaspoon cinnamon

Directions:

1. Spray 6 x 6-inch baking dish lightly with cooking spray.

2. Place baking dish in air fryer basket and preheat air fryer to 330°F.

3. In a large bowl, beat eggs and sugar together with a hand mixer.

4. Add oil, pumpkin, and vanilla and mix well.

5. Sift together all dry ingredients. Add to pumpkin mixture and beat well, about 1 minute.

6. Pour batter in baking dish and cook at 330°F for 22 minutes or until toothpick inserted in center of loaf comes out clean.

Crispy Bacon

Servings: 6
Cooking Time: 20 Minutes

Ingredients:

- 12 ounces bacon

Directions:

1. Preheat the air fryer to 350°F for 3 minutes.

2. Lay out the bacon in a single layer, slightly overlapping the strips of bacon.

3. Air fry for 10 minutes or until desired crispness.

4. Repeat until all the bacon has been cooked.

Fried Pb&j

Servings: 4
Cooking Time: 8 Minutes

Ingredients:

- ½ cup cornflakes, crushed
- ¼ cup shredded coconut
- 8 slices oat nut bread or any whole-grain, oversize bread
- 6 tablespoons peanut butter
- 2 medium bananas, cut into ½-inch-thick slices
- 6 tablespoons pineapple preserves
- 1 egg, beaten

* oil for misting or cooking spray

Directions:

1. Preheat air fryer to 360°F.

2. In a shallow dish, mix together the cornflake crumbs and coconut.

3. For each sandwich, spread one bread slice with 1½ tablespoons of peanut butter. Top with banana slices. Spread another bread slice with 1½ tablespoons of preserves. Combine to make a sandwich.

4. Using a pastry brush, brush top of sandwich lightly with beaten egg. Sprinkle with about 1½ tablespoons of crumb coating, pressing it in to make it stick. Spray with oil.

5. Turn sandwich over and repeat to coat and spray the other side.

6. Cooking 2 at a time, place sandwiches in air fryer basket and cook for 6 to 7minutes or until coating is golden brown and crispy. If sandwich doesn't brown enough, spray with a little more oil and cook at 390°F for another minute.

7. Cut cooked sandwiches in half and serve warm.

Strawberry Bread

Servings: 6
Cooking Time: 28 Minutes

Ingredients:

* ½ cup frozen strawberries in juice, completely thawed (do not drain)
* 1 cup flour
* ½ cup sugar
* 1 teaspoon cinnamon
* ½ teaspoon baking soda
* ⅛ teaspoon salt
* 1 egg, beaten
* ⅓ cup oil

* cooking spray

Directions:

1. Cut any large berries into smaller pieces no larger than ½ inch.

2. Preheat air fryer to 330°F.

3. In a large bowl, stir together the flour, sugar, cinnamon, soda, and salt.

4. In a small bowl, mix together the egg, oil, and strawberries. Add to dry ingredients and stir together gently.

5. Spray 6 x 6-inch baking pan with cooking spray.

6. Pour batter into prepared pan and cook at 330°F for 28 minutes.

7. When bread is done, let cool for 10minutes before removing from pan.

Sweet Potato-cinnamon Toast

Servings: 6
Cooking Time: 8 Minutes

Ingredients:

* 1 small sweet potato, cut into ⅜-inch slices
* oil for misting
* ground cinnamon

Directions:

1. Preheat air fryer to 390°F.

2. Spray both sides of sweet potato slices with oil. Sprinkle both sides with cinnamon to taste.

3. Place potato slices in air fryer basket in a single layer.

4. Cook for 4minutes, turn, and cook for 4 more minutes or until potato slices are barely fork tender.

Seasoned Herbed Sourdough Croutons

Servings: 4
Cooking Time: 7 Minutes

Ingredients:

- 4 cups cubed sourdough bread, 1-inch cubes (about 8 ounces)
- 1 tablespoon olive oil
- 1 teaspoon fresh thyme leaves
- ¼ – ½ teaspoon salt
- freshly ground black pepper

Directions:

1. Combine all ingredients in a bowl and taste to make sure it is seasoned to your liking.
2. Preheat the air fryer to 400°F.
3. Toss the bread cubes into the air fryer and air-fry for 7 minutes, shaking the basket once or twice while they cook.
4. Serve warm or store in an airtight container.

Cinnamon Sugar Donut Holes

Servings: 12
Cooking Time: 6 Minutes

Ingredients:

- 1 cup all-purpose flour
- 6 tablespoons cane sugar, divided
- 1 teaspoon baking powder
- 3 teaspoons ground cinnamon, divided
- ¼ teaspoon salt
- 1 large egg
- 1 teaspoon vanilla extract
- 2 tablespoons melted butter

Directions:

1. Preheat the air fryer to 370°F.
2. In a small bowl, combine the flour, 2 tablespoons of the sugar, the baking powder, 1 teaspoon of the cinnamon, and the salt. Mix well.
3. In a larger bowl, whisk together the egg, vanilla extract, and butter.
4. Slowly add the dry ingredients into the wet until all the ingredients are uniformly combined. Set the bowl inside the refrigerator for at least 30 minutes.
5. Before you're ready to cook, in a small bowl, mix together the remaining 4 tablespoons of sugar and 2 teaspoons of cinnamon.
6. Liberally spray the air fryer basket with olive oil mist so the donut holes don't stick to the bottom. Note: You do not want to use parchment paper in this recipe; it may burn if your air fryer is hotter than others.
7. Remove the dough from the refrigerator and divide it into 12 equal donut holes. You can use a 1-ounce serving scoop if you have one.
8. Roll each donut hole in the sugar and cinnamon mixture; then place in the air fryer basket. Repeat until all the donut holes are covered in the sugar and cinnamon mixture.
9. When the basket is full, cook for 6 minutes. Remove the donut holes from the basket using oven-safe tongs and let cool 5 minutes. Repeat until all 12 are cooked.

Garlic Parmesan Bread Ring

Servings: 6
Cooking Time: 30 Minutes

Ingredients:

- ½ cup unsalted butter, melted
- ¼ teaspoon salt (omit if using salted butter)
- ¾ cup grated Parmesan cheese
- 3 to 4 cloves garlic, minced

- 1 tablespoon chopped fresh parsley
- 1 pound frozen bread dough, defrosted
- olive oil
- 1 egg, beaten

Directions:

1. Combine the melted butter, salt, Parmesan cheese, garlic and chopped parsley in a small bowl.

2. Roll the dough out into a rectangle that measures 8 inches by 17 inches. Spread the butter mixture over the dough, leaving a half-inch border un-buttered along one of the long edges. Roll the dough from one long edge to the other, ending with the un-buttered border. Pinch the seam shut tightly. Shape the log into a circle sealing the ends together by pushing one end into the other and stretching the dough around it.

3. Cut out a circle of aluminum foil that is the same size as the air fryer basket. Brush the foil circle with oil and place an oven safe ramekin or glass in the center. Transfer the dough ring to the aluminum foil circle, around the ramekin. This will help you make sure the dough will fit in the basket and maintain its ring shape. Use kitchen shears to cut 8 slits around the outer edge of the dough ring halfway to the center. Brush the dough ring with egg wash.

4. Preheat the air fryer to 400°F for 4 minutes. When it has Preheated, brush the sides of the basket with oil and transfer the dough ring, foil circle and ramekin into the basket. Slide the drawer back into the air fryer, but do not turn the air fryer on. Let the dough rise inside the warm air fryer for 30 minutes.

5. After the bread has proofed in the air fryer for 30 minutes, set the temperature to 340°F and air-fry the bread ring for 15 minutes. Flip the bread over by inverting it onto a plate or cutting board and sliding it back into the air fryer basket. Air-fry for another 15 minutes. Let the bread cool for a few minutes before slicing the bread ring in between the slits and serving warm.

Banana Bread

Servings: 6
Cooking Time: 20 Minutes

Ingredients:

- cooking spray
- 1 cup white wheat flour
- ½ teaspoon baking powder
- ¼ teaspoon salt
- ¼ teaspoon baking soda
- 1 egg
- ½ cup mashed ripe banana
- ¼ cup plain yogurt
- ¼ cup pure maple syrup
- 2 tablespoons coconut oil
- ½ teaspoon pure vanilla extract

Directions:

1. Preheat air fryer to 330°F.

2. Lightly spray 6 x 6-inch baking dish with cooking spray.

3. In a medium bowl, mix together the flour, baking powder, salt, and soda.

4. In a separate bowl, beat the egg and add the mashed banana, yogurt, syrup, oil, and vanilla. Mix until well combined.

5. Pour liquid mixture into dry ingredients and stir gently to blend. Do not beat. Batter may be slightly lumpy.

6. Pour batter into baking dish and cook at 330°F for 20 minutes or until toothpick inserted in center of loaf comes out clean.

Peppered Maple Bacon Knots

Servings: 6

Cooking Time: 8 Minutes

Ingredients:

- 1 pound maple smoked center-cut bacon
- ¼ cup maple syrup
- ¼ cup brown sugar
- coarsely cracked black peppercorns

Directions:

1. Tie each bacon strip in a loose knot and place them on a baking sheet.
2. Combine the maple syrup and brown sugar in a bowl. Brush each knot generously with this mixture and sprinkle with coarsely cracked black pepper.
3. Preheat the air fryer to 390°F.
4. Air-fry the bacon knots in batches. Place one layer of knots in the air fryer basket and air-fry for 5 minutes. Turn the bacon knots over and air-fry for an additional 3 minutes.
5. Serve warm.

Oat Bran Muffins

Servings: 8

Cooking Time: 12 Minutes

Ingredients:

- ⅔ cup oat bran
- ½ cup flour
- ¼ cup brown sugar
- 1 teaspoon baking powder
- ½ teaspoon baking soda
- ⅛ teaspoon salt
- ½ cup buttermilk
- 1 egg
- 2 tablespoons canola oil
- ½ cup chopped dates, raisins, or dried cranberries
- 24 paper muffin cups
- cooking spray

Directions:

1. Preheat air fryer to 330°F.
2. In a large bowl, combine the oat bran, flour, brown sugar, baking powder, baking soda, and salt.
3. In a small bowl, beat together the buttermilk, egg, and oil.
4. Pour buttermilk mixture into bowl with dry ingredients and stir just until moistened. Do not beat.
5. Gently stir in dried fruit.
6. Use triple baking cups to help muffins hold shape during baking. Spray them with cooking spray, place 4 sets of cups in air fryer basket at a time, and fill each one ¾ full of batter.
7. Cook for 12minutes, until top springs back when lightly touched and toothpick inserted in center comes out clean.
8. Repeat for remaining muffins.

Bacon Puff Pastry Pinwheels

Servings: 8

Cooking Time: 10 Minutes

Ingredients:

- 1 sheet of puff pastry
- 2 tablespoons maple syrup
- ¼ cup brown sugar
- 8 slices bacon (not thick cut)
- coarsely cracked black pepper
- vegetable oil

Directions:

1. On a lightly floured surface, roll the puff pastry out into a square that measures roughly 10

inches wide by however long your bacon strips are (usually about 11 inches). Cut the pastry into eight even strips.

2. Brush the strips of pastry with the maple syrup and sprinkle the brown sugar on top, leaving 1 inch of dough exposed at the far end of each strip. Place a slice of bacon on each strip of puff pastry, letting 1/8-inch of the length of bacon hang over the edge of the pastry. Season generously with coarsely ground black pepper.

3. With the exposed end of the pastry strips away from you, roll the bacon and pastry strips up into pinwheels. Dab a little water on the exposed end of the pastry and pinch it to the pinwheel to seal the pastry shut.

4. Preheat the air fryer to 360°F.

5. Brush or spray the air fryer basket with a little vegetable oil. Place the pinwheels into the basket and air-fry at 360°F for 8 minutes. Turn the pinwheels over and air-fry for another 2 minutes to brown the bottom. Serve warm.

Breakfast Pot Pies

Servings: 4
Cooking Time: 20 Minutes

Ingredients:
- 1 refrigerated pie crust
- ½ pound pork breakfast sausage
- ¼ cup diced onion
- 1 garlic clove, minced
- ½ teaspoon ground black pepper
- ¼ teaspoon salt
- 1 cup chopped bell peppers
- 1 cup roasted potatoes
- 2 cups milk
- 2 to 3 tablespoons all-purpose flour

Directions:

1. Flatten the store-bought pie crust out on an even surface. Cut 4 equal circles that are slightly larger than the circumference of ramekins (by about ¼ inch). Set aside.

2. In a medium pot, sauté the breakfast sausage with the onion, garlic, black pepper, and salt. When browned, add in the bell peppers and potatoes and cook an additional 3 to 4 minutes to soften the bell peppers. Remove from the heat and portion equally into the ramekins.

3. To the same pot (without washing it), add the milk. Heat over medium-high heat until boiling. Slowly reduce to a simmer and stir in the flour, 1 tablespoon at a time, until the gravy thickens and coats the back of a wooden spoon (about 5 minutes).

4. Remove from the heat and equally portion ½ cup of gravy into each ramekin on top of the sausage and potato mixture.

5. Place the circle pie crusts on top of the ramekins, lightly pressing them down on the perimeter of each ramekin with the prongs of a fork. Gently poke the prongs into the center top of the pie crust a few times to create holes for the steam to escape as the pie cooks.

6. Bake in the air fryer for 6 minutes (or until the tops are golden brown).

7. Remove and let cool 5 minutes before serving.

Zucchini Walnut Bread

Servings: 6
Cooking Time: 30 Minutes

Ingredients:
- ¾ cup all-purpose flour
- ½ teaspoon baking soda
- 1 teaspoon ground cinnamon
- ⅛ teaspoon salt

- 1 large egg
- ⅓ cup packed brown sugar
- ¼ cup canola oil
- 1 teaspoon vanilla extract
- ⅓ cup milk
- 1 medium zucchini, shredded (about 1⅓ cups)
- ⅓ cup chopped walnuts

Directions:

1. Preheat the air fryer to 320°F.
2. In a medium bowl, mix together the flour, baking soda, cinnamon, and salt.
3. In a large bowl, whisk together the egg, brown sugar, oil, vanilla, and milk. Stir in the zucchini.
4. Slowly fold the dry ingredients into the wet ingredients. Stir in the chopped walnuts. Then pour the batter into two 4-inch oven-safe loaf pans.
5. Bake for 30 minutes or until a toothpick inserted into the center comes out clean. Let cool before slicing.
6. NOTE: Store tightly wrapped on the counter for up to 5 days, in the refrigerator for up to 10 days, or in the freezer for 3 months.

Cinnamon Biscuit Rolls

Servings: 12
Cooking Time: 5 Minutes

Ingredients:
- Dough
- ¼ cup warm water (105–115°F)
- 1 teaspoon active dry yeast
- 1 tablespoon sugar
- ½ cup buttermilk, lukewarm
- 2 cups flour, plus more for dusting
- 1 teaspoon baking powder
- ½ teaspoon salt
- 3 tablespoons cold butter
- Filling
- 1 tablespoon butter, melted
- 1 teaspoon cinnamon
- 2 tablespoons sugar
- Icing
- ⅔ cup powdered sugar
- ¼ teaspoon vanilla
- 2–3 teaspoons milk

Directions:

1. Dissolve yeast and sugar in warm water. Add buttermilk, stir, and set aside.
2. In a large bowl, sift together flour, baking powder, and salt. Using knives or a pastry blender, cut in butter until mixture is well combined and crumbly.
3. Pour in buttermilk mixture and stir with fork until a ball of dough forms.
4. Knead dough on a lightly floured surface for 5minutes. Roll into an 8 x 11-inch rectangle.
5. For the filling, spread the melted butter over the dough.
6. In a small bowl, stir together the cinnamon and sugar, then sprinkle over dough.
7. Starting on a long side, roll up dough so that you have a roll about 11 inches long. Cut into 12 slices with a serrated knife and sawing motion so slices remain round.
8. Place rolls on a plate or cookie sheet about an inch apart and let rise for 30minutes.
9. For icing, mix the powdered sugar, vanilla, and milk. Stir and add additional milk until icing reaches a good spreading consistency.
10. Preheat air fryer to 360°F.
11. Place 6 cinnamon rolls in basket and cook 5 minutes or until top springs back when lightly touched. Repeat to cook remaining 6 rolls.
12. Spread icing over warm rolls and serve.

French Toast And Turkey Sausage Roll-ups

Servings: 3

Cooking Time: 24 Minutes

Ingredients:

- 6 links turkey sausage
- 6 slices of white bread, crusts removed*
- 2 eggs
- ½ cup milk
- ½ teaspoon ground cinnamon
- ½ teaspoon vanilla extract
- 1 tablespoon butter, melted
- powdered sugar (optional)
- maple syrup

Directions:

1. Preheat the air fryer to 380°F and pour a little water into the bottom of the air fryer drawer. (This will help prevent the grease that drips into the bottom drawer from burning and smoking.)

2. Air-fry the sausage links at 380°F for 8 to 10 minutes, turning them a couple of times during the cooking process. (If you have pre-cooked sausage links, omit this step.)

3. Roll each sausage link in a piece of bread, pressing the finished seam tightly to seal shut.

4. Preheat the air fryer to 370°F.

5. Combine the eggs, milk, cinnamon, and vanilla in a shallow dish. Dip the sausage rolls in the egg mixture and let them soak in the egg for 30 seconds. Spray or brush the bottom of the air fryer basket with oil and transfer the sausage rolls to the basket, seam side down.

6. Air-fry the rolls at 370°F for 9 minutes. Brush melted butter over the bread, flip the rolls over and air-fry for an additional 5 minutes. Remove the French toast roll-ups from the basket and dust with powdered sugar, if using. Serve with maple syrup and enjoy.

Not-so-english Muffins

Servings: 4

Cooking Time: 10 Minutes

Ingredients:

- 2 strips turkey bacon, cut in half crosswise
- 2 whole-grain English muffins, split
- 1 cup fresh baby spinach, long stems removed
- ¼ ripe pear, peeled and thinly sliced
- 4 slices Provolone cheese

Directions:

1. Place bacon strips in air fryer basket and cook for 2minutes. Check and separate strips if necessary so they cook evenly. Cook for 4 more minutes, until crispy. Remove and drain on paper towels.

2. Place split muffin halves in air fryer basket and cook at 390°F for 2minutes, just until lightly browned.

3. Open air fryer and top each muffin with a quarter of the baby spinach, several pear slices, a strip of bacon, and a slice of cheese.

4. Cook at 360°F for 2minutes, until cheese completely melts.

Carrot Orange Muffins

Servings: 12

Cooking Time: 12 Minutes

Ingredients:

- 1½ cups all-purpose flour
- ½ cup granulated sugar
- ½ teaspoon ground cinnamon
- 2 teaspoons baking powder
- ¼ teaspoon baking soda
- ½ teaspoon salt

- 2 large eggs
- ¼ cup vegetable oil
- ⅓ cup orange marmalade
- 2 cups grated carrots

Directions:

1. Preheat the air fryer to 320°F.

2. In a large bowl, whisk together the flour, sugar, cinnamon, baking powder, baking soda, and salt; set aside.

3. In a separate bowl, whisk together the eggs, vegetable oil, orange marmalade, and grated carrots.

4. Make a well in the dry ingredients; then pour the wet ingredients into the well of the dry ingredients. Using a rubber spatula, mix the ingredients for 1 minute or until slightly lumpy.

5. Using silicone muffin liners, fill 6 muffin liners two-thirds full.

6. Carefully place the muffin liners in the air fryer basket and bake for 12 minutes (or until the tops are browned and a toothpick inserted in the center comes out clean). Carefully remove the muffins from the basket and repeat with remaining batter.

7. Serve warm.

Baked Eggs With Bacon-tomato Sauce

Servings: 1
Cooking Time: 12 Minutes

Ingredients:

- 1 teaspoon olive oil
- 2 tablespoons finely chopped onion
- 1 teaspoon chopped fresh oregano
- pinch crushed red pepper flakes
- 1 (14-ounce) can crushed or diced tomatoes
- salt and freshly ground black pepper
- 2 slices of bacon, chopped
- 2 large eggs
- ¼ cup grated Cheddar cheese
- fresh parsley, chopped

Directions:

1. Start by making the tomato sauce. Preheat a medium saucepan over medium heat on the stovetop. Add the olive oil and sauté the onion, oregano and pepper flakes for 5 minutes. Add the tomatoes and bring to a simmer. Season with salt and freshly ground black pepper and simmer for 10 minutes.

2. Meanwhile, Preheat the air fryer to 400°F and pour a little water into the bottom of the air fryer drawer. (This will help prevent the grease that drips into the bottom drawer from burning and smoking.) Place the bacon in the air fryer basket and air-fry at 400°F for 5 minutes, shaking the basket every once in a while.

3. When the bacon is almost crispy, remove it to a paper-towel lined plate and rinse out the air fryer drawer, draining away the bacon grease.

4. Transfer the tomato sauce to a shallow 7-inch pie dish. Crack the eggs on top of the sauce and scatter the cooked bacon back on top. Season with salt and freshly ground black pepper and transfer the pie dish into the air fryer basket. You can use an aluminum foil sling to help with this by taking a long piece of aluminum foil, folding it in half lengthwise twice until it is roughly 26-inches by 3-inches. Place this under the pie dish and hold the ends of the foil to move the pie dish in and out of the air fryer basket. Tuck the ends of the foil beside the pie dish while it cooks in the air fryer.

5. Air-fry at 400°F for 5 minutes, or until the eggs are almost cooked to your liking. Sprinkle

cheese on top and air-fry for an additional 2 minutes. When the cheese has melted, remove the pie dish from the air fryer, sprinkle with a little chopped parsley and let the eggs cool for a few minutes – just enough time to toast some buttered bread in your air fryer!

Pizza Dough

Servings: 3
Cooking Time: 10 Minutes

Ingredients:

- 4 cups bread flour, pizza ("00") flour or all-purpose flour
- 1 teaspoon active dry yeast
- 2 teaspoons sugar
- 2 teaspoons salt
- 1½ cups water
- 1 tablespoon olive oil

Directions:

1. Combine the flour, yeast, sugar and salt in the bowl of a stand mixer. Add the olive oil to the flour mixture and start to mix using the dough hook attachment. As you're mixing, add 1¼ cups of the water, mixing until the dough comes together. Continue to knead the dough with the dough hook for another 10 minutes, adding enough water to the dough to get it to the right consistency.

2. Transfer the dough to a floured counter and divide it into 3 equal portions. Roll each portion into a ball. Lightly coat each dough ball with oil and transfer to the refrigerator, covered with plastic wrap. You can place them all on a baking sheet, or place each dough ball into its own oiled zipper sealable plastic bag or container. (You can freeze the dough balls at this stage, removing as much air as possible from the oiled bag.) Keep in the refrigerator for at least one day, or as long as five days.

3. When you're ready to use the dough, remove your dough from the refrigerator at least 1 hour prior to baking and let it sit on the counter, covered gently with plastic wrap.

Quiche Cups

Servings: 10
Cooking Time: 16 Minutes

Ingredients:

- ¼ pound all-natural ground pork sausage
- 3 eggs
- ¾ cup milk
- 20 foil muffin cups
- cooking spray
- 4 ounces sharp Cheddar cheese, grated

Directions:

1. Divide sausage into 3 portions and shape each into a thin patty.

2. Place patties in air fryer basket and cook 390°F for 6minutes.

3. While sausage is cooking, prepare the egg mixture. A large measuring cup or bowl with a pouring lip works best. Combine the eggs and milk and whisk until well blended. Set aside.

4. When sausage has cooked fully, remove patties from basket, drain well, and use a fork to crumble the meat into small pieces.

5. Double the foil cups into 10 sets. Remove paper liners from the top muffin cups and spray the foil cups lightly with cooking spray.

6. Divide crumbled sausage among the 10 muffin cup sets.

7. Top each with grated cheese, divided evenly among the cups.

8. Place 5 cups in air fryer basket.

9. Pour egg mixture into each cup, filling until each cup is at least ⅔ full.

10. Cook for 8 minutes and test for doneness. A knife inserted into the center shouldn't have any raw egg on it when removed.

11. If needed, cook 2 more minutes, until egg completely sets.

12. Repeat steps 8 through 11 for the remaining quiches.

Egg And Sausage Crescent Rolls

Servings: 8

Cooking Time: 11 Minutes

Ingredients:

- 5 large eggs
- ¼ teaspoon black pepper
- ¼ teaspoon salt
- 1 tablespoon milk
- ¼ cup shredded cheddar cheese
- One 8-ounce package refrigerated crescent rolls
- 4 tablespoon pesto sauce
- 8 fully cooked breakfast sausage links, defrosted

Directions:

1. Preheat the air fryer to 320°F.

2. In a medium bowl, crack the eggs and whisk with the pepper, salt, and milk. Pour into a frying pan over medium heat and scramble. Just before the eggs are done, turn off the heat and add in the cheese. Continue to cook until the cheese has melted and the eggs are finished (about 5 minutes total). Remove from the heat.

3. Remove the crescent rolls from the package and press them flat onto a clean surface lightly dusted with flour. Add 1½ teaspoons of pesto sauce across the center of each roll. Place equal portions of eggs across all 8 rolls. Then top each roll with a sausage link and roll the dough up tight so it resembles the crescent-roll shape.

4. Lightly spray your air fryer basket with olive oil mist and place the rolls on top. Bake for 6 minutes or until the tops of the rolls are lightly browned.

5. Remove and let cool 3 to 5 minutes before serving.

DESSERTS AND SWEETS

Molten Chocolate Almond Cakes

Servings: 3

Cooking Time: 13 Minutes

Ingredients:

- butter and flour for the ramekins
- 4 ounces bittersweet chocolate, chopped
- ½ cup (1 stick) unsalted butter
- 2 eggs
- 2 egg yolks
- ¼ cup sugar
- ½ teaspoon pure vanilla extract, or almond extract
- 1 tablespoon all-purpose flour
- 3 tablespoons ground almonds
- 8 to 12 semisweet chocolate discs (or 4 chunks of chocolate)
- cocoa powder or powdered sugar, for dusting
- toasted almonds, coarsely chopped

Directions:

1. Butter and flour three (6-ounce) ramekins. (Butter the ramekins and then coat the butter with flour by shaking it around in the ramekin and dumping out any excess.)

2. Melt the chocolate and butter together, either in the microwave or in a double boiler. In a separate bowl, beat the eggs, egg yolks and sugar together until light and smooth. Add the vanilla extract. Whisk the chocolate mixture into the egg mixture. Stir in the flour and ground almonds.

3. Preheat the air fryer to 330°F.

4. Transfer the batter carefully to the buttered ramekins, filling halfway. Place two or three chocolate discs in the center of the batter and then fill the ramekins to ½-inch below the top with the remaining batter. Place the ramekins into the air fryer basket and air-fry at 330°F for 13 minutes. The sides of the cake should be set, but the centers should be slightly soft. Remove the ramekins from the air fryer and let the cakes sit for 5 minutes. (If you'd like the cake a little less molten, air-fry for 14 minutes and let the cakes sit for 4 minutes.)

5. Run a butter knife around the edge of the ramekins and invert the cakes onto a plate. Lift the ramekin off the plate slowly and carefully so that the cake doesn't break. Dust with cocoa powder or powdered sugar and serve with a scoop of ice cream and some coarsely chopped toasted almonds.

Giant Buttery Chocolate Chip Cookie

Servings: 4

Cooking Time: 16 Minutes

Ingredients:

- ⅔ cup plus 1 tablespoon All-purpose flour
- ¼ teaspoon Baking soda
- ¼ teaspoon Table salt
- Baking spray (see the headnote)
- 4 tablespoons (¼ cup/½ stick) plus 1 teaspoon Butter, at room temperature
- ¼ cup plus 1 teaspoon Packed dark brown sugar
- 3 tablespoons plus 1 teaspoon Granulated white sugar
- 2½ tablespoons Pasteurized egg substitute, such as Egg Beaters
- ½ teaspoon Vanilla extract

- ¾ cup plus 1 tablespoon Semisweet or bittersweet chocolate chips

Directions:

1. Preheat the air fryer to 350°F .

2. Whisk the flour, baking soda, and salt in a bowl until well combined.

3. For a small air fryer, coat the inside of a 6-inch round cake pan with baking spray. For a medium air fryer, coat the inside of a 7-inch round cake pan with baking spray. And for a large air fryer, coat the inside of an 8-inch round cake pan with baking spray.

4. Using a hand electric mixer at medium speed, beat the butter, brown sugar, and granulated white sugar in a bowl until smooth and thick, about 3 minutes, scraping down the inside of the bowl several times.

5. Beat in the pasteurized egg substitute or egg (as applicable) and vanilla until uniform. Scrape down and remove the beaters. Fold in the flour mixture and chocolate chips with a rubber spatula, just until combined. Scrape and gently press this dough into the prepared pan, getting it even across the pan to the perimeter.

6. Set the pan in the basket and air-fry undisturbed for 16 minutes, or until the cookie is puffed, browned, and feels set to the touch.

7. Transfer the pan to a wire rack and cool for 10 minutes. Loosen the cookie from the perimeter with a spatula, then invert the pan onto a cutting board and let the cookie come free. Remove the pan and reinvert the cookie onto the wire rack. Cool for 5 minutes more before slicing into wedges to serve.

Coconut Crusted Bananas With Pineapple Sauce

Servings: 4

Cooking Time: 5 Minutes

Ingredients:

- Pineapple Sauce
- 1½ cups puréed fresh pineapple
- 2 tablespoons sugar
- juice of 1 lemon
- ¼ teaspoon ground cinnamon
- 3 firm bananas
- ¼ cup sweetened condensed milk
- 1¼ cups shredded coconut
- ⅓ cup crushed graham crackers (crumbs)*
- vegetable or canola oil, in a spray bottle
- vanilla frozen yogurt or ice cream

Directions:

1. Make the pineapple sauce by combining the pineapple, sugar, lemon juice and cinnamon in a saucepan. Simmer the mixture on the stovetop for 20 minutes, and then set it aside.

2. Slice the bananas diagonally into ½-inch thick slices and place them in a bowl. Pour the sweetened condensed milk into the bowl and toss the bananas gently to coat. Combine the coconut and graham cracker crumbs together in a shallow dish. Remove the banana slices from the condensed milk and let any excess milk drip off. Dip the banana slices in the coconut and crumb mixture to coat both sides. Spray the coated slices with oil.

3. Preheat the air fryer to 400°F.

4. Grease the bottom of the air fryer basket with a little oil. Air-fry the bananas in batches at 400°F for 5 minutes, turning them over halfway through

the cooking time. Air-fry until the bananas are golden brown on both sides.

5. Serve warm over vanilla frozen yogurt with some of the pineapple sauce spooned over top.

Boston Cream Donut Holes

Servings: 24
Cooking Time: 12 Minutes

Ingredients:

- 1½ cups bread flour
- 1 teaspoon active dry yeast
- 1 tablespoon sugar
- ¼ teaspoon salt
- ½ cup warm milk
- ½ teaspoon pure vanilla extract
- 2 egg yolks
- 2 tablespoons butter, melted
- vegetable oil
- Custard Filling:
- 1 (3.4-ounce) box French vanilla instant pudding mix
- ¾ cup whole milk
- ¼ cup heavy cream
- Chocolate Glaze:
- 1 cup chocolate chips
- ⅓ cup heavy cream

Directions:

1. Combine the flour, yeast, sugar and salt in the bowl of a stand mixer. Add the milk, vanilla, egg yolks and butter. Mix until the dough starts to come together in a ball. Transfer the dough to a floured surface and knead the dough by hand for 2 minutes. Shape the dough into a ball, place it in a large oiled bowl, cover the bowl with a clean kitchen towel and let the dough rise for 1 to 1½ hours or until the dough has doubled in size.

2. When the dough has risen, punch it down and roll it into a 24-inch log. Cut the dough into 24 pieces and roll each piece into a ball. Place the dough balls on a baking sheet and let them rise for another 30 minutes.

3. Preheat the air fryer to 400°F.

4. Spray or brush the dough balls lightly with vegetable oil and air-fry eight at a time for 4 minutes, turning them over halfway through the cooking time.

5. While donut holes are cooking, make the filling and chocolate glaze. To make the filling, use an electric hand mixer to beat the French vanilla pudding, milk and ¼ cup of heavy cream together for 2 minutes.

6. To make the chocolate glaze, place the chocolate chips in a medium-sized bowl. Bring the heavy cream to a boil on the stovetop and pour it over the chocolate chips. Stir until the chips are melted and the glaze is smooth.

7. To fill the donut holes, place the custard filling in a pastry bag with a long tip. Poke a hole into the side of the donut hole with a small knife. Wiggle the knife around to make room for the filling. Place the pastry bag tip into the hole and slowly squeeze the custard into the center of the donut. Dip the top half of the donut into the chocolate glaze, letting any excess glaze drip back into the bowl. Let the glazed donut holes sit for a few minutes before serving.

Hasselback Apple Crisp

Servings: 4
Cooking Time: 20 Minutes

Ingredients:

- 2 large Gala apples, peeled, cored and cut in half

- ¼ cup butter, melted
- ½ teaspoon ground cinnamon
- 2 tablespoons sugar
- Topping
- 3 tablespoons butter, melted
- 2 tablespoons brown sugar
- ¼ cup chopped pecans
- 2 tablespoons rolled oats*
- 1 tablespoon flour*
- vanilla ice cream
- caramel sauce

Directions:

1. Place the apples cut side down on a cutting board. Slicing from stem end to blossom end, make 8 to 10 slits down the apple halves but only slice three quarters of the way through the apple, not all the way through to the cutting board.

2. Preheat the air fryer to 330°F and pour a little water into the bottom of the air fryer drawer. (This will help prevent the grease that drips into the bottom drawer from burning and smoking.)

3. Transfer the apples to the air fryer basket, flat side down. Combine ¼ cup of melted butter, cinnamon and sugar in a small bowl. Brush this butter mixture onto the apples and air-fry at 330°F for 15 minutes. Baste the apples several times with the butter mixture during the cooking process.

4. While the apples are air-frying, make the filling. Combine 3 tablespoons of melted butter with the brown sugar, pecans, rolled oats and flour in a bowl. Stir with a fork until the mixture resembles small crumbles.

5. When the timer on the air fryer is up, spoon the topping down the center of the apples. Air-fry at 330°F for an additional 5 minutes.

6. Transfer the apples to a serving plate and serve with vanilla ice cream and caramel sauce.

Cinnamon Sugar Banana Rolls

Servings: 6
Cooking Time: 8 Minutes

Ingredients:

- ¼ cup Granulated white sugar
- 2 teaspoons Ground cinnamon
- 2 tablespoons Peach or apricot jam or orange marmalade
- 6 Spring roll wrappers, thawed if necessary
- 2 Ripe banana(s), peeled and cut into 3-inch-long sections
- 1 Large egg, well beaten
- Vegetable oil spray

Directions:

1. Preheat the air fryer to 400°F.

2. Stir the sugar and cinnamon in a small bowl until well combined. Stir the jam or marmalade with a fork to loosen it up.

3. Set a spring roll wrapper on a clean, dry work surface. Roll a banana section in the sugar mixture until evenly and well coated. Set the coated banana along one edge of the wrapper. Top it with about 1 teaspoon of the jam or marmalade. Fold the sides of the wrapper perpendicular to the banana up and over the banana, partially covering it. Brush beaten egg over the side of the wrapper farthest from the banana. Starting with the banana, roll the wrapper closed, ending at the part with the beaten egg. Press gently to seal. Set the roll aside seam side down and continue filling and rolling the remaining wrappers in the same way.

4. Lightly coat the wrappers with vegetable oil spray. Set them seam side down in the basket

with as much air space between them as possible. Air-fry undisturbed for 8 minutes, or until crisp and golden brown.

5. Use kitchen tongs to gently transfer the rolls to a wire rack. Cool for at least 5 minutes or up to 30 minutes before serving.

Struffoli

Servings: X
Cooking Time: 20 Minutes

Ingredients:

- ¼ cup butter, softened
- ⅔ cup sugar
- 5 eggs
- 2 teaspoons vanilla extract
- zest of 1 lemon
- 4 cups all-purpose flour
- 2 teaspoons baking soda
- ¼ teaspoon salt
- 16 ounces honey
- 1 teaspoon ground cinnamon
- zest of 1 orange
- 2 tablespoons water
- nonpareils candy sprinkles

Directions:

1. Cream the butter and sugar together in a bowl until light and fluffy using a hand mixer (or a stand mixer). Add the eggs, vanilla and lemon zest and mix. In a separate bowl, combine the flour, baking soda and salt. Add the dry ingredients to the wet ingredients and mix until you have a soft dough. Shape the dough into a ball, wrap it in plastic and let it rest for 30 minutes.

2. Divide the dough ball into four pieces. Roll each piece into a long rope. Cut each rope into about 25 (½-inch) pieces. Roll each piece into a tight ball. You should have 100 little balls when finished.

3. Preheat the air fryer to 370°F.

4. In batches of about 20, transfer the dough balls to the air fryer basket, leaving a small space in between them. Air-fry the dough balls at 370°F for 3 to 4 minutes, shaking the basket when one minute of cooking time remains.

5. After all the dough balls are air-fried, make the honey topping. Melt the honey in a small saucepan on the stovetop. Add the cinnamon, orange zest, and water. Simmer for one minute. Place the air-fried dough balls in a large bowl and drizzle the honey mixture over top. Gently toss to coat all the dough balls evenly. Transfer the coated struffoli to a platter and sprinkle the nonpareil candy sprinkles over top. You can dress the presentation up by piling the balls into the shape of a wreath or pile them high in a cone shape to resemble a Christmas tree.

6. Struffoli can be made ahead. Store covered tightly.

Black And Blue Clafoutis

Servings: 2
Cooking Time: 15minutes

Ingredients:

- 6-inch pie pan
- 3 large eggs
- ½ cup sugar
- 1 teaspoon vanilla extract
- 2 tablespoons butter, melted 1 cup milk
- ½ cup all-purpose flour*
- 1 cup blackberries
- 1 cup blueberries
- 2 tablespoons confectioners' sugar

Directions:

1.   Preheat the air fryer to 320°F.

2.   Combine the eggs and sugar in a bowl and whisk vigorously until smooth, lighter in color and well combined. Add the vanilla extract, butter and milk and whisk together well. Add the flour and whisk just until no lumps or streaks of white remain.

3.   Scatter half the blueberries and blackberries in a greased (6-inch) pie pan or cake pan. Pour half of the batter (about 1¼ cups) on top of the berries and transfer the tart pan to the air fryer basket. You can use an aluminum foil sling to help with this by taking a long piece of aluminum foil, folding it in half lengthwise twice until it is roughly 26-inches by 3-inches. Place this under the pie dish and hold the ends of the foil to move the pie dish in and out of the air fryer basket. Tuck the ends of the foil beside the pie dish while it cooks in the air fryer.

4.   Air-fry at 320°F for 15 minutes or until the clafoutis has puffed up and is still a little jiggly in the center. Remove the clafoutis from the air fryer, invert it onto a plate and let it cool while you bake the second batch. Serve the clafoutis warm, dusted with confectioners' sugar on top.

Giant Vegan Chocolate Chip Cookie

Servings: 4
Cooking Time: 16 Minutes

Ingredients:
- ⅔ cup All-purpose flour
- 5 tablespoons Rolled oats (not quick-cooking or steel-cut oats)
- ¼ teaspoon Baking soda
- ¼ teaspoon Table salt
- 5 tablespoons Granulated white sugar
- ¼ cup Vegetable oil
- 2½ tablespoons Tahini (see here)
- 2½ tablespoons Maple syrup
- 2 teaspoons Vanilla extract
- ⅔ cup Vegan semisweet or bittersweet chocolate chips
- Baking spray

Directions:
1.   Preheat the air fryer to 325°F (or 330°F, if that's the closest setting).

2.   Whisk the flour, oats, baking soda, and salt in a bowl until well combined.

3.   Using an electric hand mixer at medium speed, beat the sugar, oil, tahini, maple syrup, and vanilla until rich and creamy, about 3 minutes, scraping down the inside of the bowl occasionally.

4.   Scrape down and remove the beaters. Fold in the flour mixture and chocolate chips with a rubber spatula just until all the flour is moistened and the chocolate chips are even throughout the dough.

5.   For a small air fryer, coat the inside of a 6-inch round cake pan with baking spray. For a medium air fryer, coat the inside of a 7-inch round cake pan with baking spray. And for a large air fryer, coat the inside of an 8-inch round cake pan with baking spray. Scrape and gently press the dough into the prepared pan, spreading it into an even layer to the perimeter.

6.   Set the pan in the basket and air-fry undisturbed for 16 minutes, or until puffed, browned, and firm to the touch.

7.   Transfer the pan to a wire rack and cool for 10 minutes. Loosen the cookie from the perimeter with a spatula, then invert the pan onto a cutting board and let the cookie come free. Remove the pan and reinvert the cookie onto the wire rack. Cool for 5 minutes more before slicing into wedges to serve.

Gingerbread

Servings: 6
Cooking Time: 20 Minutes

Ingredients:

- cooking spray
- 1 cup flour
- 2 tablespoons sugar
- ¾ teaspoon ground ginger
- ¼ teaspoon cinnamon
- 1 teaspoon baking powder
- ½ teaspoon baking soda
- ⅛ teaspoon salt
- 1 egg
- ¼ cup molasses
- ½ cup buttermilk
- 2 tablespoons oil
- 1 teaspoon pure vanilla extract

Directions:

1. Preheat air fryer to 330°F.
2. Spray 6 x 6-inch baking dish lightly with cooking spray.
3. In a medium bowl, mix together all the dry ingredients.
4. In a separate bowl, beat the egg. Add molasses, buttermilk, oil, and vanilla and stir until well mixed.
5. Pour liquid mixture into dry ingredients and stir until well blended.
6. Pour batter into baking dish and cook at 330°F for 20minutes or until toothpick inserted in center of loaf comes out clean.

Mixed Berry Hand Pies

Servings: 4
Cooking Time: 15 Minutes

Ingredients:

- ¾ cup sugar
- ½ teaspoon ground cinnamon
- 1 tablespoon cornstarch
- 1 cup blueberries
- 1 cup blackberries
- 1 cup raspberries, divided
- 1 teaspoon water
- 1 package refrigerated pie dough (or your own homemade pie dough)
- 1 egg, beaten

Directions:

1. Combine the sugar, cinnamon, and cornstarch in a small saucepan. Add the blueberries, blackberries, and ½ cup of the raspberries. Toss the berries gently to coat them evenly. Add the teaspoon of water to the saucepan and turn the stovetop on to medium-high heat, stirring occasionally. Once the berries break down, release their juice and start to simmer (about 5 minutes), simmer for another couple of minutes and then transfer the mixture to a bowl, stir in the remaining ½ cup of raspberries and let it cool.
2. Preheat the air fryer to 370°F.
3. Cut the pie dough into four 5-inch circles and four 6-inch circles.
4. Spread the 6-inch circles on a flat surface. Divide the berry filling between all four circles. Brush the perimeter of the dough circles with a little water. Place the 5-inch circles on top of the filling and press the perimeter of the dough circles together to seal. Roll the edges of the bottom circle up over the top circle to make a crust around the filling. Press a fork around the crust to make decorative indentations and to seal the crust shut. Brush the pies with egg wash and sprinkle a little sugar on top. Poke a small hole in

the center of each pie with a paring knife to vent the dough.

5. Air-fry two pies at a time. Brush or spray the air fryer basket with oil and place the pies into the basket. Air-fry for 9 minutes. Turn the pies over and air-fry for another 6 minutes. Serve warm or at room temperature.

Wild Blueberry Sweet Empanadas

Servings: 12
Cooking Time: 8 Minutes

Ingredients:
- 2 cups frozen wild blueberries
- 5 tablespoons chia seeds
- ¼ cup honey
- 1 tablespoon lemon or lime juice
- ¼ cup water
- 1½ cups all-purpose flour
- 1 cup whole-wheat flour
- ½ teaspoon salt
- 1 tablespoon sugar
- ½ cup cold unsalted butter
- 1 egg
- ½ cup plus 2 tablespoons milk, divided
- 1 cup powdered sugar
- 1 teaspoon vanilla extract

Directions:
1. To make the wild blueberry chia jam, place the blueberries, chia seeds, honey, lemon or lime juice, and water into a blender and pulse for 2 minutes. Pour the chia jam into a glass jar or bowl and cover. Store in the refrigerator at least 4 to 8 hours or until the jam is thickened.
2. In a food processor, place the all-purpose flour, whole-wheat flour, salt, sugar, and butter and process for 2 minutes, scraping down the sides of the food processor every 30 seconds. Add in the egg and blend for 30 seconds. Using the pulse button, add in ½ cup of the milk 1 tablespoon at a time or until the dough is moist enough to handle and be rolled into a ball. Let the dough rest at room temperature for 30 minutes.
3. On a floured surface, cut the dough in half; then form a ball and cut each ball into 6 equal pieces, totaling 12 equal pieces. Work with one piece at a time, and cover the remaining dough with a towel. Roll out the dough into a 6-inch round, much like a tortilla, with ¼ inch thickness. Place 4 tablespoons of filling in the center of round, fold over to form a half-circle. Using a fork, crimp the edges together and pierce the top with a fork for air holes. Repeat with the remaining dough and filling.
4. Preheat the air fryer to 350°F.
5. Working in batches, place 3 to 4 empanadas in the air fryer basket and spray with cooking spray. Cook for 8 minutes. Repeat in batches, as needed. Allow the sweet empanadas to cool for 15 minutes. Meanwhile, in a small bowl, whisk together the powdered sugar, the remaining 2 tablespoons of milk, and the vanilla extract. Then drizzle the glaze over the surface and serve.

Coconut-custard Pie

Servings: 4
Cooking Time: 20 Minutes

Ingredients:
- 1 cup milk
- ¼ cup plus 2 tablespoons sugar
- ¼ cup biscuit baking mix
- 1 teaspoon vanilla
- 2 eggs
- 2 tablespoons melted butter

- cooking spray
- ½ cup shredded, sweetened coconut

Directions:

1. Place all ingredients except coconut in a medium bowl.

2. Using a hand mixer, beat on high speed for 3minutes.

3. Let sit for 5minutes.

4. Preheat air fryer to 330°F.

5. Spray a 6-inch round or 6 x 6-inch square baking pan with cooking spray and place pan in air fryer basket.

6. Pour filling into pan and sprinkle coconut over top.

7. Cook pie at 330°F for 20 minutes or until center sets.

Puff Pastry Apples

Servings: 4
Cooking Time: 10 Minutes

Ingredients:

- 3 Rome or Gala apples, peeled
- 2 tablespoons sugar
- 1 teaspoon all-purpose flour
- 1 teaspoon ground cinnamon
- ⅛ teaspoon ground ginger
- pinch ground nutmeg
- 1 sheet puff pastry
- 1 tablespoon butter, cut into 4 pieces
- 1 egg, beaten
- vegetable oil
- vanilla ice cream (optional)
- caramel sauce (optional)

Directions:

1. Remove the core from the apple by cutting the four sides off the apple around the core. Slice the pieces of apple into thin half-moons, about ¼-inch thick. Combine the sugar, flour, cinnamon, ginger, and nutmeg in a large bowl. Add the apples to the bowl and gently toss until the apples are evenly coated with the spice mixture. Set aside.

2. Cut the puff pastry sheet into a 12-inch by 12-inch square. Then quarter the sheet into four 6-inch squares. Save any remaining pastry for decorating the apples at the end.

3. Divide the spiced apples between the four puff pastry squares, stacking the apples in the center of each square and placing them flat on top of each other in a circle. Top the apples with a piece of the butter.

4. Brush the four edges of the pastry with the egg wash. Bring the four corners of the pastry together, wrapping them around the apple slices and pinching them together at the top in the style of a "beggars purse" appetizer. Fold the ends of the pastry corners down onto the apple making them look like leaves. Brush the entire apple with the egg wash.

5. Using the leftover dough, make leaves to decorate the apples. Cut out 8 leaf shapes, about 1½-inches long, "drawing" the leaf veins on the pastry leaves with a paring knife. Place 2 leaves on the top of each apple, tucking the ends of the leaves under the pastry in the center of the apples. Brush the top of the leaves with additional egg wash. Sprinkle the entire apple with some granulated sugar.

6. Preheat the air fryer to 350°F.

7. Spray or brush the inside of the air fryer basket with oil. Place the apples in the basket and air-fry for 6 minutes. Carefully turn the apples over – it's easiest to remove one apple, then flip

the others over and finally return the last apple to the air fryer. Air-fry for an additional 4 minutes.

8. Serve the puff pastry apples warm with vanilla ice cream and drizzle with some caramel sauce.

White Chocolate Cranberry Blondies

Servings: 6
Cooking Time: 18 Minutes

Ingredients:
- ⅓ cup butter
- ½ cup sugar
- 1 teaspoon vanilla extract
- 1 large egg
- 1 cup all-purpose flour
- ½ teaspoon baking powder
- ⅛ teaspoon salt
- ¼ cup dried cranberries
- ¼ cup white chocolate chips

Directions:
1. Preheat the air fryer to 320°F.
2. In a large bowl, cream the butter with the sugar and vanilla extract. Whisk in the egg and set aside.
3. In a separate bowl, mix the flour with the baking powder and salt. Then gently mix the dry ingredients into the wet. Fold in the cranberries and chocolate chips.
4. Liberally spray an oven-safe 7-inch springform pan with olive oil and pour the batter into the pan.
5. Cook for 17 minutes or until a toothpick inserted in the center comes out clean.
6. Remove and let cool 5 minutes before serving.

Easy Churros

Servings: 12
Cooking Time: 10 Minutes

Ingredients:
- ½ cup Water
- 4 tablespoons (¼ cup/½ stick) Butter
- ¼ teaspoon Table salt
- ½ cup All-purpose flour
- 2 Large egg(s)
- ¼ cup Granulated white sugar
- 2 teaspoons Ground cinnamon

Directions:
1. Bring the water, butter, and salt to a boil in a small saucepan set over high heat, stirring occasionally.
2. When the butter has fully melted, reduce the heat to medium and stir in the flour to form a dough. Continue cooking, stirring constantly, to dry out the dough until it coats the bottom and sides of the pan with a film, even a crust. Remove the pan from the heat, scrape the dough into a bowl, and cool for 15 minutes.
3. Using an electric hand mixer at medium speed, beat in the egg, or eggs one at a time, until the dough is smooth and firm enough to hold its shape.
4. Mix the sugar and cinnamon in a small bowl. Scoop up 1 tablespoon of the dough and roll it in the sugar mixture to form a small, coated tube about ½ inch in diameter and 2 inches long. Set it aside and make 5 more tubes for the small batch or 11 more for the large one.
5. Set the tubes on a plate and freeze for 20 minutes. Meanwhile, Preheat the air fryer to 375°F .
6. Set 3 frozen tubes in the basket for a small batch or 6 for a large one with as much air space between them as possible. Air-fry undisturbed for 10 minutes, or until puffed, brown, and set.

7. Use kitchen tongs to transfer the churros to a wire rack to cool for at least 5 minutes. Meanwhile, air-fry and cool the second batch of churros in the same way.

Annie's Chocolate Chunk Hazelnut Cookies

Servings: 24
Cooking Time: 12 Minutes

Ingredients:

- 1 cup butter, softened
- 1 cup brown sugar
- ½ cup granulated sugar
- 2 eggs, lightly beaten
- 1½ teaspoons vanilla extract
- 1½ cups all-purpose flour
- ½ cup rolled oats
- 1 teaspoon baking soda
- ½ teaspoon salt
- 2 cups chocolate chunks
- ½ cup toasted chopped hazelnuts

Directions:

1. Cream the butter and sugars together until light and fluffy using a stand mixer or electric hand mixer. Add the eggs and vanilla, and beat until well combined.

2. Combine the flour, rolled oats, baking soda and salt in a second bowl. Gradually add the dry ingredients to the wet ingredients with a wooden spoon or spatula. Stir in the chocolate chunks and hazelnuts until distributed throughout the dough.

3. Shape the cookies into small balls about the size of golf balls and place them on a baking sheet. Freeze the cookie balls for at least 30 minutes, or package them in as airtight a package as you can and keep them in your freezer.

4. When you're ready for a delicious snack or dessert, Preheat the air fryer to 350°F. Cut a piece of parchment paper to fit the number of cookies you are baking. Place the parchment down in the air fryer basket and place the frozen cookie ball or balls on top (remember to leave room for them to expand).

5. Air-fry the cookies at 350°F for 12 minutes, or until they are done to your liking. Let them cool for a few minutes before enjoying your freshly baked cookie.

Baked Apple

Servings: 6
Cooking Time: 20 Minutes

Ingredients:

- 3 small Honey Crisp or other baking apples
- 3 tablespoons maple syrup
- 3 tablespoons chopped pecans
- 1 tablespoon firm butter, cut into 6 pieces

Directions:

1. Put ½ cup water in the drawer of the air fryer.
2. Wash apples well and dry them.
3. Split apples in half. Remove core and a little of the flesh to make a cavity for the pecans.
4. Place apple halves in air fryer basket, cut side up.
5. Spoon 1½ teaspoons pecans into each cavity.
6. Spoon ½ tablespoon maple syrup over pecans in each apple.
7. Top each apple with ½ teaspoon butter.
8. Cook at 360°F for 20 minutes, until apples are tender.

Midnight Nutella® Banana Sandwich

Servings: 2
Cooking Time: 8 Minutes

Ingredients:
- butter, softened
- 4 slices white bread*
- ¼ cup chocolate hazelnut spread (Nutella®)
- 1 banana

Directions:
1. Preheat the air fryer to 370°F.
2. Spread the softened butter on one side of all the slices of bread and place the slices buttered side down on the counter. Spread the chocolate hazelnut spread on the other side of the bread slices. Cut the banana in half and then slice each half into three slices lengthwise. Place the banana slices on two slices of bread and top with the remaining slices of bread (buttered side up) to make two sandwiches. Cut the sandwiches in half (triangles or rectangles) – this will help them all fit in the air fryer at once. Transfer the sandwiches to the air fryer.
3. Air-fry at 370°F for 5 minutes. Flip the sandwiches over and air-fry for another 2 to 3 minutes, or until the top bread slices are nicely browned. Pour yourself a glass of milk or a midnight nightcap while the sandwiches cool slightly and enjoy!

Chocolate Macaroons

Servings: 16
Cooking Time: 8 Minutes

Ingredients:
- 2 Large egg white(s), at room temperature
- ⅛ teaspoon Table salt
- ½ cup Granulated white sugar
- 1½ cups Unsweetened shredded coconut
- 3 tablespoons Unsweetened cocoa powder

Directions:
1. Preheat the air fryer to 375°F .
2. Using an electric mixer at high speed, beat the egg white(s) and salt in a medium or large bowl until stiff peaks can be formed when the turned-off beaters are dipped into the mixture.
3. Still working with the mixer at high speed, beat in the sugar in a slow stream until the meringue is shiny and thick.
4. Scrape down and remove the beaters. Fold in the coconut and cocoa with a rubber spatula until well combined, working carefully to deflate the meringue as little as possible.
5. Scoop up 2 tablespoons of the mixture. Wet your clean hands and roll that little bit of coconut bliss into a ball. Set it aside and continue making more balls: 7 more for a small batch, 15 more for a medium batch, or 23 more for a large one.
6. Line the bottom of the machine's basket or the basket attachment with parchment paper. Set the balls on the parchment with as much air space between them as possible. Air-fry undisturbed for 8 minutes, or until dry, set, and lightly browned.
7. Use a nonstick-safe spatula to transfer the macaroons to a wire rack. Cool for at least 10 minutes before serving. Or cool to room temperature, about 30 minutes, then store in a sealed container at room temperature for up to 3 days.

Brown Sugar Baked Apples

Servings: 4

Cooking Time: 15 Minutes

Ingredients:

- 3 Small tart apples, preferably McIntosh
- 4 tablespoons (¼ cup/½ stick) Butter
- 6 tablespoons Light brown sugar
- Ground cinnamon
- Table salt

Directions:

1. Preheat the air fryer to 400°F.

2. Stem the apples, then cut them in half through their "equators" (that is, not the stem ends). Use a melon baller to core the apples, taking care not to break through the flesh and skin at any point but creating a little well in the center of each half.

3. When the machine is at temperature, remove the basket and set it on a heat-safe work surface. Set the apple halves cut side up in the basket with as much air space between them as possible. Even a fraction of an inch will work. Drop 2 teaspoons of butter into the well in the center of each apple half. Sprinkle each half with 1 tablespoon brown sugar and a pinch each ground cinnamon and table salt.

4. Return the basket to the machine. Air-fry undisturbed for 15 minutes, or until the apple halves have softened and the brown sugar has caramelized.

5. Use a nonstick-safe spatula to transfer the apple halves cut side up to a wire rack. Cool for at least 10 minutes before serving, or serve at room temperature.

Giant Oatmeal–peanut Butter Cookie

Servings: 4

Cooking Time: 18 Minutes

Ingredients:

- 1 cup Rolled oats (not quick-cooking or steel-cut oats)
- ½ cup All-purpose flour
- ½ teaspoon Ground cinnamon
- ½ teaspoon Baking soda
- ⅓ cup Packed light brown sugar
- ¼ cup Solid vegetable shortening
- 2 tablespoons Natural-style creamy peanut butter
- 3 tablespoons Granulated white sugar
- 2 tablespoons (or 1 small egg, well beaten) Pasteurized egg substitute, such as Egg Beaters
- ⅓ cup Roasted, salted peanuts, chopped
- Baking spray

Directions:

1. Preheat the air fryer to 350°F .

2. Stir the oats, flour, cinnamon, and baking soda in a bowl until well combined.

3. Using an electric hand mixer at medium speed, beat the brown sugar, shortening, peanut butter, granulated white sugar, and egg substitute or egg (as applicable) until smooth and creamy, about 3 minutes, scraping down the inside of the bowl occasionally.

4. Scrape down and remove the beaters. Fold in the flour mixture and peanuts with a rubber spatula just until all the flour is moistened and the peanut bits are evenly distributed in the dough.

5. For a small air fryer, coat the inside of a 6-inch round cake pan with baking spray. For a medium air fryer, coat the inside of a 7-inch

round cake pan with baking spray. And for a large air fryer, coat the inside of an 8-inch round cake pan with baking spray. Scrape and gently press the dough into the prepared pan, spreading it into an even layer to the perimeter.

6. Set the pan in the basket and air-fry undisturbed for 18 minutes, or until well browned.

7. Transfer the pan to a wire rack and cool for 15 minutes. Loosen the cookie from the perimeter with a spatula, then invert the pan onto a cutting board and let the cookie come free. Remove the pan and reinvert the cookie onto the wire rack. Cool for 5 minutes more before slicing into wedges to serve.

One-bowl Chocolate Buttermilk Cake

Servings: 6
Cooking Time: 16-20 Minutes

Ingredients:
- ¾ cup All-purpose flour
- ½ cup Granulated white sugar
- 3 tablespoons Unsweetened cocoa powder
- ½ teaspoon Baking soda
- ¼ teaspoon Table salt
- ½ cup Buttermilk
- 2 tablespoons Vegetable oil
- ¾ teaspoon Vanilla extract
- Baking spray (see here)

Directions:
1. Preheat the air fryer to 325°F (or 330°F, if that's the closest setting).

2. Stir the flour, sugar, cocoa powder, baking soda, and salt in a large bowl until well combined. Add the buttermilk, oil, and vanilla. Stir just until a thick, grainy batter forms.

3. Use the baking spray to generously coat the inside of a 6-inch round cake pan for a small batch, a 7-inch round cake pan for a medium batch, or an 8-inch round cake pan for a large batch. Scrape and spread the chocolate batter into this pan, smoothing the batter out to an even layer.

4. Set the pan in the basket and air-fry undisturbed for 16 minutes for a 6-inch layer, 18 minutes for a 7-inch layer, or 20 minutes for an 8-inch layer, or until a toothpick or cake tester inserted into the center of the cake comes out clean. Start checking it at the 14-minute mark to know where you are.

5. Use hot pads or silicone baking mitts to transfer the cake pan to a wire rack. Cool for 5 minutes. To unmold, set a cutting board over the baking pan and invert both the board and the pan. Lift the still-warm pan off the cake layer. Set the wire rack on top of the cake layer and invert all of it with the cutting board so that the cake layer is now right side up on the wire rack. Remove the cutting board and continue cooling the cake for at least 10 minutes or to room temperature, about 30 minutes, before slicing into wedges.

Giant Buttery Oatmeal Cookie

Servings: 4
Cooking Time: 16 Minutes

Ingredients:
- 1 cup Rolled oats (not quick-cooking or steel-cut oats)
- ½ cup All-purpose flour
- ½ teaspoon Baking soda
- ½ teaspoon Ground cinnamon
- ½ teaspoon Table salt
- 3½ tablespoons Butter, at room temperature
- ⅓ cup Packed dark brown sugar
- 1½ tablespoons Granulated white sugar
- 3 tablespoons (or 1 medium egg, well beaten) Pasteurized egg substitute, such as Egg Beaters
- ¾ teaspoon Vanilla extract

- ⅓ cup Chopped pecans
- Baking spray

Directions:

1. Preheat the air fryer to 350°F .
2. Stir the oats, flour, baking soda, cinnamon, and salt in a bowl until well combined.
3. Using an electric hand mixer at medium speed , beat the butter, brown sugar, and granulated white sugar until creamy and thick, about 3 minutes, scraping down the inside of the bowl occasionally. Beat in the egg substitute or egg (as applicable) and vanilla until uniform.
4. Scrape down and remove the beaters. Fold in the flour mixture and pecans with a rubber spatula just until all the flour is moistened and the nuts are even throughout the dough.
5. For a small air fryer, coat the inside of a 6-inch round cake pan with baking spray. For a medium air fryer, coat the inside of a 7-inch round cake pan with baking spray. And for a large air fryer, coat the inside of an 8-inch round cake pan with baking spray. Scrape and gently press the dough into the prepared pan, spreading it into an even layer to the perimeter.
6. Set the pan in the basket and air-fry undisturbed for 16 minutes, or until puffed and browned.
7. Transfer the pan to a wire rack and cool for 10 minutes. Loosen the cookie from the perimeter with a spatula, then invert the pan onto a cutting board and let the cookie come free. Remove the pan and reinvert the cookie onto the wire rack. Cool for 5 minutes more before slicing into wedges to serve.

Peanut Butter S'mores

Servings:10
Cooking Time: 1 Minute

Ingredients:

- 10 Graham crackers (full, double-square cookies as they come out of the package)
- 5 tablespoons Natural-style creamy or crunchy peanut butter
- ½ cup Milk chocolate chips
- 10 Standard-size marshmallows (not minis and not jumbo campfire ones)

Directions:

1. Preheat the air fryer to 350°F .
2. Break the graham crackers in half widthwise at the marked place, so the rectangle is now in two squares. Set half of the squares flat side up on your work surface. Spread each with about 1½ teaspoons peanut butter, then set 10 to 12 chocolate chips point side up into the peanut butter on each, pressing gently so the chips stick.
3. Flatten a marshmallow between your clean, dry hands and set it atop the chips. Do the same with the remaining marshmallows on the other coated graham crackers. Do not set the other half of the graham crackers on top of these coated graham crackers.
4. When the machine is at temperature, set the treats graham cracker side down in a single layer in the basket. They may touch, but even a fraction of an inch between them will provide better air flow. Air-fry undisturbed for 45 seconds.
5. Use a nonstick-safe spatula to transfer the topped graham crackers to a wire rack. Set the other graham cracker squares flat side down over the marshmallows. Cool for a couple of minutes before serving.

VEGETARIANS RECIPES

Thai Peanut Veggie Burgers

Servings: 6
Cooking Time: 14 Minutes

Ingredients:

- One 15.5-ounce can cannellini beans
- 1 teaspoon minced garlic
- ¼ cup chopped onion
- 1 Thai chili pepper, sliced
- 2 tablespoons natural peanut butter
- ½ teaspoon black pepper
- ½ teaspoon salt
- ⅓ cup all-purpose flour (optional)
- ½ cup cooked quinoa
- 1 large carrot, grated
- 1 cup shredded red cabbage
- ¼ cup peanut dressing
- ¼ cup chopped cilantro
- 6 Hawaiian rolls
- 6 butterleaf lettuce leaves

Directions:

1. Preheat the air fryer to 350°F.
2. To a blender or food processor fitted with a metal blade, add the beans, garlic, onion, chili pepper, peanut butter, pepper, and salt. Pulse for 5 to 10 seconds. Do not over process. The mixture should be coarse, not smooth.
3. Remove from the blender or food processor and spoon into a large bowl. Mix in the cooked quinoa and carrots. At this point, the mixture should begin to hold together to form small patties. If the dough appears to be too sticky (meaning you likely processed a little too long), add the flour to hold the patties together.
4. Using a large spoon, form 8 equal patties out of the batter.
5. Liberally spray a metal trivet with olive oil spray and set in the air fryer basket. Place the patties into the basket, leaving enough space to be able to turn them with a spatula.
6. Cook for 7 minutes, flip, and cook another 7 minutes.
7. Remove from the heat and repeat with additional patties.
8. To serve, place the red cabbage in a bowl and toss with peanut dressing and cilantro. Place the veggie burger on a bun, and top with a slice of lettuce and cabbage slaw.

Mexican Twice Air-fried Sweet Potatoes

Servings: 2
Cooking Time: 42 Minutes

Ingredients:

- 2 large sweet potatoes
- olive oil
- salt and freshly ground black pepper
- ⅓ cup diced red onion
- ⅓ cup diced red bell pepper
- ½ cup canned black beans, drained and rinsed
- ½ cup corn kernels, fresh or frozen
- ½ teaspoon chili powder
- 1½ cups grated pepper jack cheese, divided
- Jalapeño peppers, sliced

Directions:

1. Preheat the air fryer to 400°F.
2. Rub the outside of the sweet potatoes with olive oil and season with salt and freshly ground

black pepper. Transfer the potatoes into the air fryer basket and air-fry at 400°F for 30 minutes, rotating the potatoes a few times during the cooking process.

3. While the potatoes are air-frying, start the potato filling. Preheat a large sauté pan over medium heat on the stovetop. Add the onion and pepper and sauté for a few minutes, until the vegetables start to soften. Add the black beans, corn, and chili powder and sauté for another 3 minutes. Set the mixture aside.

4. Remove the sweet potatoes from the air fryer and let them rest for 5 minutes. Slice off one inch of the flattest side of both potatoes. Scrape the potato flesh out of the potatoes, leaving half an inch of potato flesh around the edge of the potato. Place all the potato flesh into a large bowl and mash it with a fork. Add the black bean mixture and 1 cup of the pepper jack cheese to the mashed sweet potatoes. Season with salt and freshly ground black pepper and mix well. Stuff the hollowed out potato shells with the black bean and sweet potato mixture, mounding the filling high in the potatoes.

5. Transfer the stuffed potatoes back into the air fryer basket and air-fry at 370°F for 10 minutes. Sprinkle the remaining cheese on top of each stuffed potato, lower the heat to 340°F and air-fry for an additional 2 minutes to melt the cheese. Top with a couple slices of Jalapeño pepper and serve warm with a green salad.

Charred Cauliflower Tacos

Servings: 4
Cooking Time: 10 Minutes
Ingredients:

- 1 head cauliflower, washed and cut into florets
- 2 tablespoons avocado oil
- 2 teaspoons taco seasoning
- 1 medium avocado
- ½ teaspoon garlic powder
- ¼ teaspoon black pepper
- ¼ teaspoon salt
- 2 tablespoons chopped red onion
- 2 teaspoons fresh squeezed lime juice
- ¼ cup chopped cilantro
- Eight 6-inch corn tortillas
- ½ cup cooked corn
- ½ cup shredded purple cabbage

Directions:
1. Preheat the air fryer to 390°F.
2. In a large bowl, toss the cauliflower with the avocado oil and taco seasoning. Set the metal trivet inside the air fryer basket and liberally spray with olive oil.
3. Place the cauliflower onto the trivet and cook for 10 minutes, shaking every 3 minutes to allow for an even char.
4. While the cauliflower is cooking, prepare the avocado sauce. In a medium bowl, mash the avocado; then mix in the garlic powder, pepper, salt, and onion. Stir in the lime juice and cilantro; set aside.
5. Remove the cauliflower from the air fryer basket.
6. Place 1 tablespoon of avocado sauce in the middle of a tortilla, and top with corn, cabbage, and charred cauliflower. Repeat with the remaining tortillas. Serve immediately.

Cheesy Enchilada Stuffed Baked Potatoes

Servings: 4

Cooking Time: 37 Minutes

Ingredients:

- 2 medium russet potatoes, washed
- One 15-ounce can mild red enchilada sauce
- One 15-ounce can low-sodium black beans, rinsed and drained
- 1 teaspoon taco seasoning
- ½ cup shredded cheddar cheese
- 1 medium avocado, halved
- ½ teaspoon garlic powder
- ¼ teaspoon black pepper
- ¼ teaspoon salt
- 2 teaspoons fresh lime juice
- 2 tablespoon chopped red onion
- ¼ cup chopped cilantro

Directions:

1. Preheat the air fryer to 390°F.
2. Puncture the outer surface of the potatoes with a fork.
3. Set the potatoes inside the air fryer basket and cook for 20 minutes, rotate, and cook another 10 minutes.
4. In a large bowl, mix the enchilada sauce, black beans, and taco seasoning.
5. When the potatoes have finished cooking, carefully remove them from the air fryer basket and let cool for 5 minutes.
6. Using a pair of tongs to hold the potato if it's still too hot to touch, slice the potato in half lengthwise. Use a spoon to scoop out the potato flesh and add it into the bowl with the enchilada sauce. Mash the potatoes with the enchilada sauce mixture, creating a uniform stuffing.
7. Place the potato skins into an air-fryer-safe pan and stuff the halves with the enchilada stuffing. Sprinkle the cheese over the top of each potato.
8. Set the air fryer temperature to 350°F, return the pan to the air fryer basket, and cook for another 5 to 7 minutes to heat the potatoes and melt the cheese.
9. While the potatoes are cooking, take the avocado and scoop out the flesh into a small bowl. Mash it with the back of a fork; then mix in the garlic powder, pepper, salt, lime juice, and onion. Set aside.
10. When the potatoes have finished cooking, remove the pan from the air fryer and place the potato halves on a plate. Top with avocado mash and fresh cilantro. Serve immediately.

Spaghetti Squash And Kale Fritters With Pomodoro Sauce

Servings: 3

Cooking Time: 45 Minutes

Ingredients:

- 1½-pound spaghetti squash (about half a large or a whole small squash)
- olive oil
- ½ onion, diced
- ½ red bell pepper, diced
- 2 cloves garlic, minced
- 4 cups coarsely chopped kale
- salt and freshly ground black pepper
- 1 egg
- ⅓ cup breadcrumbs, divided*
- ⅓ cup grated Parmesan cheese
- ½ teaspoon dried rubbed sage
- pinch nutmeg
- Pomodoro Sauce:

- 2 tablespoons olive oil
- ½ onion, chopped
- 1 to 2 cloves garlic, minced
- 1 (28-ounce) can peeled tomatoes
- ¼ cup red wine
- 1 teaspoon Italian seasoning
- 2 tablespoons chopped fresh basil, plus more for garnish
- salt and freshly ground black pepper
- ½ teaspoon sugar (optional)

Directions:

1. Preheat the air fryer to 370°F.
2. Cut the spaghetti squash in half lengthwise and remove the seeds. Rub the inside of the squash with olive oil and season with salt and pepper. Place the squash, cut side up, into the air fryer basket and air-fry for 30 minutes, flipping the squash over halfway through the cooking process.
3. While the squash is cooking, Preheat a large sauté pan over medium heat on the stovetop. Add a little olive oil and sauté the onions for 3 minutes, until they start to soften. Add the red pepper and garlic and continue to sauté for an additional 4 minutes. Add the kale and season with salt and pepper. Cook for 2 more minutes, or until the kale is soft. Transfer the mixture to a large bowl and let it cool.
4. While the squash continues to cook, make the Pomodoro sauce. Preheat the large sauté pan again over medium heat on the stovetop. Add the olive oil and sauté the onion and garlic for 2 to 3 minutes, until the onion begins to soften. Crush the canned tomatoes with your hands and add them to the pan along with the red wine and Italian seasoning and simmer for 20 minutes. Add the basil and season to taste with salt, pepper and sugar (if using).
5. When the spaghetti squash has finished cooking, use a fork to scrape the inside flesh of the squash onto a sheet pan. Spread the squash out and let it cool.
6. Once cool, add the spaghetti squash to the kale mixture, along with the egg, breadcrumbs, Parmesan cheese, sage, nutmeg, salt and freshly ground black pepper. Stir to combine well and then divide the mixture into 6 thick portions. You can shape the portions into patties, but I prefer to keep them a little random and unique in shape. Spray or brush the fritters with olive oil.
7. Preheat the air fryer to 370°F.
8. Brush the air fryer basket with a little olive oil and transfer the fritters to the basket. Air-fry the squash and kale fritters at 370°F for 15 minutes, flipping them over halfway through the cooking process.
9. Serve the fritters warm with the Pomodoro sauce spooned over the top or pooled on your plate. Garnish with the fresh basil leaves.

Broccoli Cheddar Stuffed Potatoes

Servings: 2
Cooking Time: 42 Minutes

Ingredients:

- 2 large russet potatoes, scrubbed
- 1 tablespoon olive oil
- salt and freshly ground black pepper
- 2 tablespoons butter
- ¼ cup sour cream
- 3 tablespoons half-and-half (or milk)
- 1¼ cups grated Cheddar cheese, divided
- ¾ teaspoon salt

- freshly ground black pepper
- 1 cup frozen baby broccoli florets, thawed and drained

Directions:

1. Preheat the air fryer to 400°F.
2. Rub the potatoes all over with olive oil and season generously with salt and freshly ground black pepper. Transfer the potatoes into the air fryer basket and air-fry for 30 minutes, turning the potatoes over halfway through the cooking process.
3. Remove the potatoes from the air fryer and let them rest for 5 minutes. Cut a large oval out of the top of both potatoes. Leaving half an inch of potato flesh around the edge of the potato, scoop the inside of the potato out and into a large bowl to prepare the potato filling. Mash the scooped potato filling with a fork and add the butter, sour cream, half-and-half, 1 cup of the grated Cheddar cheese, salt and pepper to taste. Mix well and then fold in the broccoli florets.
4. Stuff the hollowed out potato shells with the potato and broccoli mixture. Mound the filling high in the potatoes – you will have more filling than room in the potato shells.
5. Transfer the stuffed potatoes back to the air fryer basket and air-fry at 360°F for 10 minutes. Sprinkle the remaining Cheddar cheese on top of each stuffed potato, lower the heat to 330°F and air-fry for an additional minute or two to melt cheese.

Pinto Taquitos

Servings: 4
Cooking Time: 8 Minutes

Ingredients:

- 12 corn tortillas (6- to 7-inch size)
- Filling
- ½ cup refried pinto beans
- ½ cup grated sharp Cheddar or Pepper Jack cheese
- ¼ cup corn kernels (if frozen, measure after thawing and draining)
- 2 tablespoons chopped green onion
- 2 tablespoons chopped jalapeño pepper (seeds and ribs removed before chopping)
- ½ teaspoon lime juice
- ½ teaspoon chile powder, plus extra for dusting
- ½ teaspoon cumin
- ½ teaspoon garlic powder
- oil for misting or cooking spray
- salsa, sour cream, or guacamole for dipping

Directions:

1. Mix together all filling Ingredients.
2. Warm refrigerated tortillas for easier rolling. (Wrap in damp paper towels and microwave for 30 to 60 seconds.)
3. Working with one at a time, place 1 tablespoon of filling on tortilla and roll up. Spray with oil or cooking spray and dust outside with chile powder to taste.
4. Place 6 taquitos in air fryer basket (4 on bottom layer, 2 stacked crosswise on top). Cook at 390°F for 8 minutes, until crispy and brown.
5. Repeat step 4 to cook remaining taquitos.
6. Serve plain or with salsa, sour cream, or guacamole for dipping.

Vegetable Couscous

Servings: 4
Cooking Time: 10 Minutes

Ingredients:

- 4 ounces white mushrooms, sliced
- ½ medium green bell pepper, julienned
- 1 cup cubed zucchini
- ¼ small onion, slivered
- 1 stalk celery, thinly sliced
- ¼ teaspoon ground coriander
- ¼ teaspoon ground cumin
- salt and pepper
- 1 tablespoon olive oil
- Couscous
- ¾ cup uncooked couscous
- 1 cup vegetable broth or water
- ½ teaspoon salt (omit if using salted broth)

Directions:

1. Combine all vegetables in large bowl. Sprinkle with coriander, cumin, and salt and pepper to taste. Stir well, add olive oil, and stir again to coat vegetables evenly.

2. Place vegetables in air fryer basket and cook at 390°F for 5minutes. Stir and cook for 5 more minutes, until tender.

3. While vegetables are cooking, prepare the couscous: Place broth or water and salt in large saucepan. Heat to boiling, stir in couscous, cover, and remove from heat.

4. Let couscous sit for 5minutes, stir in cooked vegetables, and serve hot.

Egg Rolls

Servings: 4
Cooking Time: 8 Minutes

Ingredients:

- 1 clove garlic, minced
- 1 teaspoon sesame oil
- 1 teaspoon olive oil
- ½ cup chopped celery
- ½ cup grated carrots
- 2 green onions, chopped
- 2 ounces mushrooms, chopped
- 2 cups shredded Napa cabbage
- 1 teaspoon low-sodium soy sauce
- 1 teaspoon cornstarch
- salt
- 1 egg
- 1 tablespoon water
- 4 egg roll wraps
- olive oil for misting or cooking spray

Directions:

1. In a large skillet, sauté garlic in sesame and olive oils over medium heat for 1 minute.

2. Add celery, carrots, onions, and mushrooms to skillet. Cook 1 minute, stirring.

3. Stir in cabbage, cover, and cook for 1 minute or just until cabbage slightly wilts.

4. In a small bowl, mix soy sauce and cornstarch. Stir into vegetables to thicken. Remove from heat. Salt to taste if needed.

5. Beat together egg and water in a small bowl.

6. Divide filling into 4 portions and roll up in egg roll wraps. Brush all over with egg wash to seal.

7. Mist egg rolls very lightly with olive oil or cooking spray and place in air fryer basket.

8. Cook at 390°F for 4minutes. Turn over and cook 4 more minutes, until golden brown and crispy.

Parmesan Portobello Mushroom Caps

Servings: 2

Cooking Time: 14 Minutes

Ingredients:

- ¼ cup flour*
- 1 egg, lightly beaten
- 1 cup seasoned breadcrumbs*
- 2 large portobello mushroom caps, stems and gills removed
- olive oil, in a spray bottle
- ½ cup tomato sauce
- ¾ cup grated mozzarella cheese
- 1 tablespoon grated Parmesan cheese
- 1 tablespoon chopped fresh basil or parsley

Directions:

1. Set up a dredging station with three shallow dishes. Place the flour in the first shallow dish, egg in the second dish and breadcrumbs in the last dish. Dredge the mushrooms in flour, then dip them into the egg and finally press them into the breadcrumbs to coat on all sides. Spray both sides of the coated mushrooms with olive oil.

2. Preheat the air fryer to 400°F.

3. Air-fry the mushrooms at 400°F for 10 minutes, turning them over halfway through the cooking process.

4. Fill the underside of the mushrooms with the tomato sauce and then top the sauce with the mozzarella and Parmesan cheeses. Reset the air fryer temperature to 350°F and air-fry for an additional 4 minutes, until the cheese has melted and is slightly browned.

5. Serve the mushrooms with pasta tossed with tomato sauce and garnish with some chopped fresh basil or parsley.

Corn And Pepper Jack Chile Rellenos With Roasted Tomato Sauce

Servings: 3

Cooking Time: 30 Minutes

Ingredients:

- 3 Poblano peppers
- 1 cup all-purpose flour*
- salt and freshly ground black pepper
- 2 eggs, lightly beaten
- 1 cup plain breadcrumbs*
- olive oil, in a spray bottle
- Sauce
- 2 cups cherry tomatoes
- 1 Jalapeño pepper, halved and seeded
- 1 clove garlic
- ¼ red onion, broken into large pieces
- 1 tablespoon olive oil
- salt, to taste
- 2 tablespoons chopped fresh cilantro
- Filling
- olive oil
- ¼ red onion, finely chopped
- 1 teaspoon minced garlic
- 1 cup corn kernels, fresh or frozen
- 2 cups grated pepper jack cheese

Directions:

1. Start by roasting the peppers. Preheat the air fryer to 400°F. Place the peppers into the air fryer basket and air-fry at 400°F for 10 minutes, turning them over halfway through the cooking time. Remove the peppers from the basket and cover loosely with foil.

2. While the peppers are cooling, make the roasted tomato sauce. Place all sauce Ingredients except for the cilantro into the air fryer basket and

air-fry at 400°F for 10 minutes, shaking the basket once or twice. When the sauce Ingredients have finished air-frying, transfer everything to a blender or food processor and blend or process to a smooth sauce, adding a little warm water to get the desired consistency. Season to taste with salt, add the cilantro and set aside.

3. While the sauce Ingredients are cooking in the air fryer, make the filling. Heat a skillet on the stovetop over medium heat. Add the olive oil and sauté the red onion and garlic for 4 to 5 minutes. Transfer the onion and garlic to a bowl, stir in the corn and cheese, and set aside.

4. Set up a dredging station with three shallow dishes. Place the flour, seasoned with salt and pepper, in the first shallow dish. Place the eggs in the second dish, and fill the third shallow dish with the breadcrumbs. When the peppers have cooled, carefully slice into one side of the pepper to create an opening. Pull the seeds out of the peppers and peel away the skins, trying not to tear the pepper. Fill each pepper with some of the corn and cheese filling and close the pepper up again by folding one side of the opening over the other. Carefully roll each pepper in the seasoned flour, then into the egg and finally into the breadcrumbs to coat on all sides, trying not to let the pepper fall open. Spray the peppers on all sides with a little olive oil.

5. Air-fry two peppers at a time at 350°F for 6 minutes. Turn the peppers over and air-fry for another 4 minutes. Serve the peppers warm on a bed of the roasted tomato sauce.

Veggie Fried Rice

Servings: 4
Cooking Time: 25 Minutes

Ingredients:
- 1 cup cooked brown rice
- ⅓ cup chopped onion
- ½ cup chopped carrots
- ½ cup chopped bell peppers
- ½ cup chopped broccoli florets
- 3 tablespoons low-sodium soy sauce
- 1 tablespoon sesame oil
- 1 teaspoon ground ginger
- 1 teaspoon ground garlic powder
- ½ teaspoon black pepper
- ⅛ teaspoon salt
- 2 large eggs

Directions:
1. Preheat the air fryer to 370°F.
2. In a large bowl, mix together the brown rice, onions, carrots, bell pepper, and broccoli.
3. In a small bowl, whisk together the soy sauce, sesame oil, ginger, garlic powder, pepper, salt, and eggs.
4. Pour the egg mixture into the rice and vegetable mixture and mix together.
5. Liberally spray a 7-inch springform pan (or compatible air fryer dish) with olive oil. Add the rice mixture to the pan and cover with aluminum foil.
6. Place a metal trivet into the air fryer basket and set the pan on top. Cook for 15 minutes. Carefully remove the pan from basket, discard the foil, and mix the rice. Return the rice to the air fryer basket, turning down the temperature to 350°F and cooking another 10 minutes.
7. Remove and let cool 5 minutes. Serve warm.

Spicy Vegetable And Tofu Shake Fry

Servings: 4

Cooking Time: 17 Minutes

Ingredients:

- 4 teaspoons canola oil, divided
- 2 tablespoons rice wine vinegar
- 1 tablespoon sriracha chili sauce
- ¼ cup soy sauce*
- ½ teaspoon toasted sesame oil
- 1 teaspoon minced garlic
- 1 tablespoon minced fresh ginger
- 8 ounces extra firm tofu
- ½ cup vegetable stock or water
- 1 tablespoon honey
- 1 tablespoon cornstarch
- ½ red onion, chopped
- 1 red or yellow bell pepper, chopped
- 1 cup green beans, cut into 2-inch lengths
- 4 ounces mushrooms, sliced
- 2 scallions, sliced
- 2 tablespoons fresh cilantro leaves
- 2 teaspoons toasted sesame seeds

Directions:

1. Combine 1 tablespoon of the oil, vinegar, sriracha sauce, soy sauce, sesame oil, garlic and ginger in a small bowl. Cut the tofu into bite-sized cubes and toss the tofu in with the marinade while you prepare the other vegetables. When you are ready to start cooking, remove the tofu from the marinade and set it aside. Add the water, honey and cornstarch to the marinade and bring to a simmer on the stovetop, just until the sauce thickens. Set the sauce aside.

2. Preheat the air fryer to 400°F.

3. Toss the onion, pepper, green beans and mushrooms in a bowl with a little canola oil and season with salt. Air-fry at 400°F for 11 minutes, shaking the basket and tossing the vegetables every few minutes. When the vegetables are cooked to your preferred doneness, remove them from the air fryer and set aside.

4. Add the tofu to the air fryer basket and air-fry at 400°F for 6 minutes, shaking the basket a few times during the cooking process. Add the vegetables back to the basket and air-fry for another minute. Transfer the vegetables and tofu to a large bowl, add the scallions and cilantro leaves and toss with the sauce. Serve over rice with sesame seeds sprinkled on top.

Cauliflower Steaks Gratin

Servings: 2

Cooking Time: 13 Minutes

Ingredients:

- 1 head cauliflower
- 1 tablespoon olive oil
- salt and freshly ground black pepper
- ½ teaspoon chopped fresh thyme leaves
- 3 tablespoons grated Parmigiano-Reggiano cheese
- 2 tablespoons panko breadcrumbs

Directions:

1. Preheat the air-fryer to 370°F.

2. Cut two steaks out of the center of the cauliflower. To do this, cut the cauliflower in half and then cut one slice about 1-inch thick off each half. The rest of the cauliflower will fall apart into florets, which you can roast on their own or save for another meal.

3. Brush both sides of the cauliflower steaks with olive oil and season with salt, freshly ground

black pepper and fresh thyme. Place the cauliflower steaks into the air fryer basket and air-fry for 6 minutes. Turn the steaks over and air-fry for another 4 minutes. Combine the Parmesan cheese and panko breadcrumbs and sprinkle the mixture over the tops of both steaks and air-fry for another 3 minutes until the cheese has melted and the breadcrumbs have browned. Serve this with some sautéed bitter greens and air-fried blistered tomatoes.

Asparagus, Mushroom And Cheese Soufflés

Servings: 3
Cooking Time: 21 Minutes

Ingredients:
- butter
- grated Parmesan cheese
- 3 button mushrooms, thinly sliced
- 8 spears asparagus, sliced ½-inch long
- 1 teaspoon olive oil
- 1 tablespoon butter
- 4½ teaspoons flour
- pinch paprika
- pinch ground nutmeg
- salt and freshly ground black pepper
- ½ cup milk
- ½ cup grated Gruyère cheese or other Swiss cheese (about 2 ounces)
- 2 eggs, separated

Directions:
1. Butter three 6-ounce ramekins and dust with grated Parmesan cheese. (Butter the ramekins and then coat the butter with Parmesan by shaking it around in the ramekin and dumping out any excess.)
2. Preheat the air fryer to 400°F.

3. Toss the mushrooms and asparagus in a bowl with the olive oil. Transfer the vegetables to the air fryer and air-fry for 7 minutes, shaking the basket once or twice to redistribute the Ingredients while they cook.
4. While the vegetables are cooking, make the soufflé base. Melt the butter in a saucepan on the stovetop over medium heat. Add the flour, stir and cook for a minute or two. Add the paprika, nutmeg, salt and pepper. Whisk in the milk and bring the mixture to a simmer to thicken. Remove the pan from the heat and add the cheese, stirring to melt. Let the mixture cool for just a few minutes and then whisk the egg yolks in, one at a time. Stir in the cooked mushrooms and asparagus. Let this soufflé base cool.
5. In a separate bowl, whisk the egg whites to soft peak stage (the point at which the whites can almost stand up on the end of your whisk). Fold the whipped egg whites into the soufflé base, adding a little at a time.
6. Preheat the air fryer to 330°F.
7. Transfer the batter carefully to the buttered ramekins, leaving about ½-inch at the top. Place the ramekins into the air fryer basket and air-fry for 14 minutes. The soufflés should have risen nicely and be brown on top. Serve immediately.

Basic Fried Tofu

Servings: 4
Cooking Time: 17 Minutes

Ingredients:
- 14 ounces extra-firm tofu, drained and pressed
- 1 tablespoon sesame oil
- 2 tablespoons low-sodium soy sauce
- ¼ cup rice vinegar

- 1 tablespoon fresh grated ginger
- 1 clove garlic, minced
- 3 tablespoons cornstarch
- ¼ teaspoon black pepper
- ⅛ teaspoon salt

Directions:

1. Cut the tofu into 16 cubes. Set aside in a glass container with a lid.

2. In a medium bowl, mix the sesame oil, soy sauce, rice vinegar, ginger, and garlic. Pour over the tofu and secure the lid. Place in the refrigerator to marinate for an hour.

3. Preheat the air fryer to 350°F.

4. In a small bowl, mix the cornstarch, black pepper, and salt.

5. Transfer the tofu to a large bowl and discard the leftover marinade. Pour the cornstarch mixture over the tofu and toss until all the pieces are coated.

6. Liberally spray the air fryer basket with olive oil mist and set the tofu pieces inside. Allow space between the tofu so it can cook evenly. Cook in batches if necessary.

7. Cook 15 to 17 minutes, shaking the basket every 5 minutes to allow the tofu to cook evenly on all sides. When it's done cooking, the tofu will be crisped and browned on all sides.

8. Remove the tofu from the air fryer basket and serve warm.

Quinoa Burgers With Feta Cheese And Dill

Servings: 6
Cooking Time: 10 Minutes

Ingredients:

- 1 cup quinoa (red, white or multi-colored)
- 1½ cups water
- 1 teaspoon salt
- freshly ground black pepper
- 1½ cups rolled oats
- 3 eggs, lightly beaten
- ¼ cup minced white onion
- ½ cup crumbled feta cheese
- ¼ cup chopped fresh dill
- salt and freshly ground black pepper
- vegetable or canola oil, in a spray bottle
- whole-wheat hamburger buns (or gluten-free hamburger buns*)
- arugula
- tomato, sliced
- red onion, sliced
- mayonnaise

Directions:

1. Make the quinoa: Rinse the quinoa in cold water in a saucepan, swirling it with your hand until any dry husks rise to the surface. Drain the quinoa as well as you can and then put the saucepan on the stovetop to dry and toast the quinoa. Turn the heat to medium-high and shake the pan regularly until you see the quinoa moving easily and can hear the seeds moving in the pan, indicating that they are dry. Add the water, salt and pepper. Bring the liquid to a boil and then reduce the heat to low or medium-low. You should see just a few bubbles, not a boil. Cover with a lid, leaving it askew and simmer for 20 minutes. Turn the heat off and fluff the quinoa with a fork. If there's any liquid left in the bottom of the pot, place it back on the burner for another 3 minutes or so. Spread the cooked quinoa out on a sheet pan to cool.

2. Combine the room temperature quinoa in a large bowl with the oats, eggs, onion, cheese and dill. Season with salt and pepper and mix well

(remember that feta cheese is salty). Shape the mixture into 6 patties with flat sides (so they fit more easily into the air fryer). Add a little water or a few more rolled oats if necessary to get the mixture to be the right consistency to make patties.

3. Preheat the air-fryer to 400°F.

4. Spray both sides of the patties generously with oil and transfer them to the air fryer basket in one layer (you will probably have to cook these burgers in batches, depending on the size of your air fryer). Air-fry each batch at 400°F for 10 minutes, flipping the burgers over halfway through the cooking time.

5. Build your burger on the whole-wheat hamburger buns with arugula, tomato, red onion and mayonnaise.

Falafels

Servings: 12
Cooking Time: 10 Minutes

Ingredients:
- 1 pouch falafel mix
- 2–3 tablespoons plain breadcrumbs
- oil for misting or cooking spray

Directions:
1. Prepare falafel mix according to package directions.
2. Preheat air fryer to 390°F.
3. Place breadcrumbs in shallow dish or on wax paper.
4. Shape falafel mixture into 12 balls and flatten slightly. Roll in breadcrumbs to coat all sides and mist with oil or cooking spray.
5. Place falafels in air fryer basket in single layer and cook for 5minutes. Shake basket, and

continue cooking for 5minutes, until they brown and are crispy.

Roasted Vegetable Lasagna

Servings: 6
Cooking Time: 55 Minutes

Ingredients:
- 1 zucchini, sliced
- 1 yellow squash, sliced
- 8 ounces mushrooms, sliced
- 1 red bell pepper, cut into 2-inch strips
- 1 tablespoon olive oil
- 2 cups ricotta cheese
- 2 cups grated mozzarella cheese, divided
- 1 egg
- 1 teaspoon salt
- freshly ground black pepper
- ¼ cup shredded carrots
- ½ cup chopped fresh spinach
- 8 lasagna noodles, cooked
- Béchamel Sauce:
- 3 tablespoons butter
- 3 tablespoons flour
- 2½ cups milk
- ½ cup grated Parmesan cheese
- ½ teaspoon salt
- freshly ground black pepper
- pinch of ground nutmeg

Directions:
1. Preheat the air fryer to 400°F.
2. Toss the zucchini, yellow squash, mushrooms and red pepper in a large bowl with the olive oil and season with salt and pepper. Air-fry for 10 minutes, shaking the basket once or twice while the vegetables cook.
3. While the vegetables are cooking, make the béchamel sauce and cheese filling. Melt the butter

in a medium saucepan over medium-high heat on the stovetop. Add the flour and whisk, cooking for a couple of minutes. Add the milk and whisk vigorously until smooth. Bring the mixture to a boil and simmer until the sauce thickens. Stir in the Parmesan cheese and season with the salt, pepper and nutmeg. Set the sauce aside.

4. Combine the ricotta cheese, 1¼ cups of the mozzarella cheese, egg, salt and pepper in a large bowl and stir until combined. Fold in the carrots and spinach.

5. When the vegetables have finished cooking, build the lasagna. Use a baking dish that is 6 inches in diameter and 4 inches high. Cover the bottom of the baking dish with a little béchamel sauce. Top with two lasagna noodles, cut to fit the dish and overlapping each other a little. Spoon a third of the ricotta cheese mixture and then a third of the roasted veggies on top of the noodles. Pour ½ cup of béchamel sauce on top and then repeat these layers two more times: noodles – cheese mixture – vegetables – béchamel sauce. Sprinkle the remaining mozzarella cheese over the top. Cover the dish with aluminum foil, tenting it loosely so the aluminum doesn't touch the cheese.

6. Lower the dish into the air fryer basket using an aluminum foil sling (fold a piece of aluminum foil into a strip about 2-inches wide by 24-inches long). Fold the ends of the aluminum foil over the top of the dish before returning the basket to the air fryer. Air-fry for 45 minutes, removing the foil for the last 2 minutes, to slightly brown the cheese on top.

7. Let the lasagna rest for at least 20 minutes to set up a little before slicing into it and serving.

Vegetable Hand Pies

Servings: 8
Cooking Time: 10 Minutes Per Batch

Ingredients:
- ¾ cup vegetable broth
- 8 ounces potatoes
- ¾ cup frozen chopped broccoli, thawed
- ¼ cup chopped mushrooms
- 1 tablespoon cornstarch
- 1 tablespoon milk
- 1 can organic flaky biscuits (8 large biscuits)
- oil for misting or cooking spray

Directions:
1. Place broth in medium saucepan over low heat.
2. While broth is heating, grate raw potato into a bowl of water to prevent browning. You will need ¾ cup grated potato.
3. Roughly chop the broccoli.
4. Drain potatoes and put them in the broth along with the broccoli and mushrooms. Cook on low for 5 minutes.
5. Dissolve cornstarch in milk, then stir the mixture into the broth. Cook about a minute, until mixture thickens a little. Remove from heat and cool slightly.
6. Separate each biscuit into 2 rounds. Divide vegetable mixture evenly over half the biscuit rounds, mounding filling in the center of each.
7. Top the four rounds with filling, then the other four rounds and crimp the edges together with a fork.
8. Spray both sides with oil or cooking spray and place 4 pies in a single layer in the air fryer basket.
9. Cook at 330°F for approximately 10 minutes.
10. Repeat with the remaining biscuits. The second batch may cook more quickly because the fryer will be hot.

Roasted Vegetable, Brown Rice And Black Bean Burrito

Servings: 2

Cooking Time: 20 Minutes

Ingredients:

- ½ zucchini, sliced ¼-inch thick
- ½ red onion, sliced
- 1 yellow bell pepper, sliced
- 2 teaspoons olive oil
- salt and freshly ground black pepper
- 2 burrito size flour tortillas
- 1 cup grated pepper jack cheese
- ½ cup cooked brown rice
- ½ cup canned black beans, drained and rinsed
- ¼ teaspoon ground cumin
- 1 tablespoon chopped fresh cilantro
- fresh salsa, guacamole and sour cream, for serving

Directions:

1. Preheat the air fryer to 400°F.

2. Toss the vegetables in a bowl with the olive oil, salt and freshly ground black pepper. Air-fry at 400°F for 12 to 15 minutes, shaking the basket a few times during the cooking process. The vegetables are done when they are cooked to your liking.

3. In the meantime, start building the burritos. Lay the tortillas out on the counter. Sprinkle half of the cheese in the center of the tortillas. Combine the rice, beans, cumin and cilantro in a bowl, season to taste with salt and freshly ground black pepper and then divide the mixture between the two tortillas. When the vegetables have finished cooking, transfer them to the two tortillas, placing the vegetables on top of the rice and beans. Sprinkle the remaining cheese on top and then roll the burritos up, tucking in the sides of the tortillas as you roll. Brush or spray the outside of the burritos with olive oil and transfer them to the air fryer.

4. Air-fry at 360°F for 8 minutes, turning them over when there are about 2 minutes left. The burritos will have slightly brown spots, but will still be pliable.

5. Serve with some fresh salsa, guacamole and sour cream.

Roasted Vegetable Thai Green Curry

Servings: 4

Cooking Time: 16 Minutes

Ingredients:

- 1 (13-ounce) can coconut milk
- 3 tablespoons green curry paste
- 1 tablespoon soy sauce*
- 1 tablespoon rice wine vinegar
- 1 teaspoon sugar
- 1 teaspoon minced fresh ginger
- ½ onion, chopped
- 3 carrots, sliced
- 1 red bell pepper, chopped
- olive oil
- 10 stalks of asparagus, cut into 2-inch pieces
- 3 cups broccoli florets
- basmati rice for serving
- fresh cilantro
- crushed red pepper flakes (optional)

Directions:

1. Combine the coconut milk, green curry paste, soy sauce, rice wine vinegar, sugar and ginger in a medium saucepan and bring to a boil on the stovetop. Reduce the heat and simmer for 20 minutes while you cook the vegetables. Set aside.

2. Preheat the air fryer to 400°F.

3. Toss the onion, carrots, and red pepper together with a little olive oil and transfer the vegetables to the air fryer basket. Air-fry at 400°F for 10 minutes, shaking the basket a few times during the cooking process. Add the asparagus and broccoli florets and air-fry for an additional 6 minutes, again shaking the basket for even cooking.

4. When the vegetables are cooked to your liking, toss them with the green curry sauce and serve in bowls over basmati rice. Garnish with fresh chopped cilantro and crushed red pepper flakes.

Spicy Sesame Tempeh Slaw With Peanut Dressing

Servings: 2

Cooking Time: 8 Minutes

Ingredients:

- 2 cups hot water
- 1 teaspoon salt
- 8 ounces tempeh, sliced into 1-inch-long pieces
- 2 tablespoons low-sodium soy sauce
- 2 tablespoons rice vinegar
- 1 tablespoon filtered water
- 2 teaspoons sesame oil
- ½ teaspoon fresh ginger
- 1 clove garlic, minced
- ¼ teaspoon black pepper
- ½ jalapeño, sliced
- 4 cups cabbage slaw
- 4 tablespoons Peanut Dressing (see the following recipe)
- 2 tablespoons fresh chopped cilantro
- 2 tablespoons chopped peanuts

Directions:

1. Mix the hot water with the salt and pour over the tempeh in a glass bowl. Stir and cover with a towel for 10 minutes.

2. Discard the water and leave the tempeh in the bowl.

3. In a medium bowl, mix the soy sauce, rice vinegar, filtered water, sesame oil, ginger, garlic, pepper, and jalapeño. Pour over the tempeh and cover with a towel. Place in the refrigerator to marinate for at least 2 hours.

4. Preheat the air fryer to 370°F. Remove the tempeh from the bowl and discard the remaining marinade.

5. Liberally spray the metal trivet that goes into the air fryer basket and place the tempeh on top of the trivet.

6. Cook for 4 minutes, flip, and cook another 4 minutes.

7. In a large bowl, mix the cabbage slaw with the Peanut Dressing and toss in the cilantro and chopped peanuts.

8. Portion onto 4 plates and place the cooked tempeh on top when cooking completes. Serve immediately.

Stuffed Zucchini Boats

Servings: 2

Cooking Time: 20 Minutes

Ingredients:

- olive oil
- ½ cup onion, finely chopped
- 1 clove garlic, finely minced
- ½ teaspoon dried oregano
- ¼ teaspoon dried thyme
- ¾ cup couscous
- 1½ cups chicken stock, divided
- 1 tomato, seeds removed and finely chopped

- ½ cup coarsely chopped Kalamata olives
- ½ cup grated Romano cheese
- ¼ cup pine nuts, toasted
- 1 tablespoon chopped fresh parsley
- 1 teaspoon salt
- freshly ground black pepper
- 1 egg, beaten
- 1 cup grated mozzarella cheese, divided
- 2 thick zucchini

Directions:

1. Preheat a sauté pan on the stovetop over medium-high heat. Add the olive oil and sauté the onion until it just starts to soften–about 4 minutes. Stir in the garlic, dried oregano and thyme. Add the couscous and sauté for just a minute. Add 1¼ cups of the chicken stock and simmer over low heat for 3 to 5 minutes, until liquid has been absorbed and the couscous is soft. Remove the pan from heat and set it aside to cool slightly.

2. Fluff the couscous and add the tomato, Kalamata olives, Romano cheese, pine nuts, parsley, salt and pepper. Mix well. Add the remaining chicken stock, the egg and ½ cup of the mozzarella cheese. Stir to ensure everything is combined.

3. Cut each zucchini in half lengthwise. Then, trim each half of the zucchini into four 5-inch lengths. (Save the trimmed ends of the zucchini for another use.) Use a spoon to scoop out the center of the zucchini, leaving some flesh around the sides. Brush both sides of the zucchini with olive oil and season the cut side with salt and pepper.

4. Preheat the air fryer to 380°F.

5. Divide the couscous filling between the four zucchini boats. Use your hands to press the filling together and fill the inside of the zucchini. The filling should be mounded into the boats and rounded on top.

6. Transfer the zucchini boats to the air fryer basket and drizzle the stuffed zucchini boats with olive oil. Air-fry for 19 minutes. Then, sprinkle the remaining mozzarella cheese on top of the zucchini, pressing it down onto the filling lightly to prevent it from blowing around in the air fryer. Air-fry for one more minute to melt the cheese. Transfer the finished zucchini boats to a serving platter and garnish with the chopped parsley.

Rigatoni With Roasted Onions, Fennel, Spinach And Lemon Pepper Ricotta

Servings: 2
Cooking Time: 13 Minutes

Ingredients:
- 1 red onion, rough chopped into large chunks
- 2 teaspoons olive oil, divided
- 1 bulb fennel, sliced ¼-inch thick
- ¾ cup ricotta cheese
- 1½ teaspoons finely chopped lemon zest, plus more for garnish
- 1 teaspoon lemon juice
- salt and freshly ground black pepper
- 8 ounces (½ pound) dried rigatoni pasta
- 3 cups baby spinach leaves

Directions:

1. Bring a large stockpot of salted water to a boil on the stovetop and Preheat the air fryer to 400°F.

2. While the water is coming to a boil, toss the chopped onion in 1 teaspoon of olive oil and transfer to the air fryer basket. Air-fry at 400°F for 5 minutes. Toss the sliced fennel with 1

teaspoon of olive oil and add this to the air fryer basket with the onions. Continue to air-fry at 400°F for 8 minutes, shaking the basket a few times during the cooking process.

3. Combine the ricotta cheese, lemon zest and juice, ¼ teaspoon of salt and freshly ground black pepper in a bowl and stir until smooth.

4. Add the dried rigatoni to the boiling water and cook according to the package directions. When the pasta is cooked al dente, reserve one cup of the pasta water and drain the pasta into a colander.

5. Place the spinach in a serving bowl and immediately transfer the hot pasta to the bowl, wilting the spinach. Add the roasted onions and fennel and toss together. Add a little pasta water to the dish if it needs moistening. Then, dollop the lemon pepper ricotta cheese on top and nestle it into the hot pasta. Garnish with more lemon zest if desired.

FISH AND SEAFOOD RECIPES

Sweet Potato–wrapped Shrimp

Servings:3
Cooking Time: 6 Minutes

Ingredients:

- 24 Long spiralized sweet potato strands
- Olive oil spray
- ¼ teaspoon Garlic powder
- ¼ teaspoon Table salt
- Up to a ⅛ teaspoon Cayenne
- 12 Large shrimp (20–25 per pound), peeled and deveined

Directions:

1. Preheat the air fryer to 400°F.
2. Lay the spiralized sweet potato strands on a large swath of paper towels and straighten out the strands to long ropes. Coat them with olive oil spray, then sprinkle them with the garlic powder, salt, and cayenne.
3. Pick up 2 strands and wrap them around the center of a shrimp, with the ends tucked under what now becomes the bottom side of the shrimp. Continue wrapping the remainder of the shrimp.
4. Set the shrimp bottom side down in the basket with as much air space between them as possible. Air-fry undisturbed for 6 minutes, or until the sweet potato strands are crisp and the shrimp are pink and firm.
5. Use kitchen tongs to transfer the shrimp to a wire rack. Cool for only a minute or two before serving.

Better Fish Sticks

Servings:3
Cooking Time: 8 Minutes

Ingredients:

- ¾ cup Seasoned Italian-style dried bread crumbs (gluten-free, if a concern)
- 3 tablespoons (about ½ ounce) Finely grated Parmesan cheese
- 10 ounces Skinless cod fillets, cut lengthwise into 1-inch-wide pieces
- 3 tablespoons Regular or low-fat mayonnaise (not fat-free; gluten-free, if a concern)
- Vegetable oil spray

Directions:

1. Preheat the air fryer to 400°F.
2. Mix the bread crumbs and grated Parmesan in a shallow soup bowl or a small pie plate.
3. Smear the fish fillet sticks completely with the mayonnaise, then dip them one by one in the bread-crumb mixture, turning and pressing gently to make an even and thorough coating. Coat each stick on all sides with vegetable oil spray.
4. Set the fish sticks in the basket with at least ¼ inch between them. Air-fry undisturbed for 8 minutes, or until golden brown and crisp.
5. Use a nonstick-safe spatula to gently transfer them from the basket to a wire rack. Cool for only a minute or two before serving.

Flounder Fillets

Servings: 4
Cooking Time: 8 Minutes

Ingredients:

- 1 egg white
- 1 tablespoon water
- 1 cup panko breadcrumbs
- 2 tablespoons extra-light virgin olive oil
- 4 4-ounce flounder fillets

- salt and pepper
- oil for misting or cooking spray

Directions:

1. Preheat air fryer to 390°F.
2. Beat together egg white and water in shallow dish.
3. In another shallow dish, mix panko crumbs and oil until well combined and crumbly (best done by hand).
4. Season flounder fillets with salt and pepper to taste. Dip each fillet into egg mixture and then roll in panko crumbs, pressing in crumbs so that fish is nicely coated.
5. Spray air fryer basket with nonstick cooking spray and add fillets. Cook at 390°F for 3minutes.
6. Spray fish fillets but do not turn. Cook 5 minutes longer or until golden brown and crispy. Using a spatula, carefully remove fish from basket and serve.

Crispy Sweet-and-sour Cod Fillets

Servings:3

Cooking Time: 12 Minutes

Ingredients:

- 1½ cups Plain panko bread crumbs (gluten-free, if a concern)
- 2 tablespoons Regular or low-fat mayonnaise (not fat-free; gluten-free, if a concern)
- ¼ cup Sweet pickle relish
- 3 4- to 5-ounce skinless cod fillets

Directions:

1. Preheat the air fryer to 400°F.
2. Pour the bread crumbs into a shallow soup plate or a small pie plate. Mix the mayonnaise and relish in a small bowl until well combined.

Smear this mixture all over the cod fillets. Set them in the crumbs and turn until evenly coated on all sides, even on the ends.

3. Set the coated cod fillets in the basket with as much air space between them as possible. They should not touch. Air-fry undisturbed for 12 minutes, or until browned and crisp.
4. Use a nonstick-safe spatula to transfer the cod pieces to a wire rack. Cool for only a minute or two before serving hot.

Pecan-crusted Tilapia

Servings: 4

Cooking Time: 8 Minutes

Ingredients:

- 1 pound skinless, boneless tilapia filets
- ¼ cup butter, melted
- 1 teaspoon minced fresh or dried rosemary
- 1 cup finely chopped pecans
- 1 teaspoon sea salt
- ¼ teaspoon paprika
- 2 tablespoons chopped parsley
- 1 lemon, cut into wedges

Directions:

1. Pat the tilapia filets dry with paper towels.
2. Pour the melted butter over the filets and flip the filets to coat them completely.
3. In a medium bowl, mix together the rosemary, pecans, salt, and paprika.
4. Preheat the air fryer to 350°F.
5. Place the tilapia filets into the air fryer basket and top with the pecan coating. Cook for 6 to 8 minutes. The fish should be firm to the touch and flake easily when fully cooked.
6. Remove the fish from the air fryer. Top the fish with chopped parsley and serve with lemon wedges.

Five Spice Red Snapper With Green Onions And Orange Salsa

Servings: 2
Cooking Time: 8 Minutes

Ingredients:

- 2 oranges, peeled, segmented and chopped
- 1 tablespoon minced shallot
- 1 to 3 teaspoons minced red Jalapeño or Serrano pepper
- 1 tablespoon chopped fresh cilantro
- lime juice, to taste
- salt, to taste
- 2 (5- to 6-ounce) red snapper fillets
- ½ teaspoon Chinese five spice powder
- salt and freshly ground black pepper
- vegetable or olive oil, in a spray bottle
- 4 green onions, cut into 2-inch lengths

Directions:

1. Start by making the salsa. Cut the peel off the oranges, slicing around the oranges to expose the flesh. Segment the oranges by cutting in between the membranes of the orange. Chop the segments roughly and combine in a bowl with the shallot, Jalapeño or Serrano pepper, cilantro, lime juice and salt. Set the salsa aside.
2. Preheat the air fryer to 400°F.
3. Season the fish fillets with the five-spice powder, salt and freshly ground black pepper. Spray both sides of the fish fillets with oil. Toss the green onions with a little oil.
4. Transfer the fish to the air fryer basket and scatter the green onions around the fish. Air-fry at 400°F for 8 minutes.
5. Remove the fish from the air fryer, along with the fried green onions. Serve with white rice and a spoonful of the salsa on top.

Salmon Croquettes

Servings: 4
Cooking Time: 8 Minutes

Ingredients:

- 1 tablespoon oil
- ½ cup breadcrumbs
- 1 14.75-ounce can salmon, drained and all skin and fat removed
- 1 egg, beaten
- ⅓ cup coarsely crushed saltine crackers (about 8 crackers)
- ½ teaspoon Old Bay Seasoning
- ½ teaspoon onion powder
- ½ teaspoon Worcestershire sauce

Directions:

1. Preheat air fryer to 390°F.
2. In a shallow dish, mix oil and breadcrumbs until crumbly.
3. In a large bowl, combine the salmon, egg, cracker crumbs, Old Bay, onion powder, and Worcestershire. Mix well and shape into 8 small patties about ½-inch thick.
4. Gently dip each patty into breadcrumb mixture and turn to coat well on all sides.
5. Cook at 390°F for 8minutes or until outside is crispy and browned.

Crab Stuffed Salmon Roast

Servings: 4
Cooking Time: 20 Minutes

Ingredients:

- 1 (1½-pound) salmon fillet
- salt and freshly ground black pepper
- 6 ounces crabmeat
- 1 teaspoon finely chopped lemon zest
- 1 teaspoon Dijon mustard

- 1 tablespoon chopped fresh parsley, plus more for garnish
- 1 scallion, chopped
- ¼ teaspoon salt
- olive oil

Directions:

1. Prepare the salmon fillet by butterflying it. Slice into the thickest side of the salmon, parallel to the countertop and along the length of the fillet. Don't slice all the way through to the other side – stop about an inch from the edge. Open the salmon up like a book. Season the salmon with salt and freshly ground black pepper.

2. Make the crab filling by combining the crabmeat, lemon zest, mustard, parsley, scallion, salt and freshly ground black pepper in a bowl. Spread this filling in the center of the salmon. Fold one side of the salmon over the filling. Then fold the other side over on top.

3. Transfer the rolled salmon to the center of a piece of parchment paper that is roughly 6- to 7-inches wide and about 12-inches long. The parchment paper will act as a sling, making it easier to put the salmon into the air fryer. Preheat the air fryer to 370°F. Use the parchment paper to transfer the salmon roast to the air fryer basket and tuck the ends of the paper down beside the salmon. Drizzle a little olive oil on top and season with salt and pepper.

4. Air-fry the salmon at 370°F for 20 minutes.

5. Remove the roast from the air fryer and let it rest for a few minutes. Then, slice it, sprinkle some more lemon zest and parsley (or fresh chives) on top and serve.

Sea Bass With Potato Scales And Caper Aïoli

Servings: 2
Cooking Time: 10 Minutes

Ingredients:
- 2 (6- to 8-ounce) fillets of sea bass
- salt and freshly ground black pepper
- ¼ cup mayonnaise
- 2 teaspoons finely chopped lemon zest
- 1 teaspoon chopped fresh thyme
- 2 fingerling potatoes, very thinly sliced into rounds
- olive oil
- ½ clove garlic, crushed into a paste
- 1 tablespoon capers, drained and rinsed
- 1 tablespoon olive oil
- 1 teaspoon lemon juice, to taste

Directions:

1. Preheat the air fryer to 400°F.

2. Season the fish well with salt and freshly ground black pepper. Mix the mayonnaise, lemon zest and thyme together in a small bowl. Spread a thin layer of the mayonnaise mixture on both fillets. Start layering rows of potato slices onto the fish fillets to simulate the fish scales. The second row should overlap the first row slightly. Dabbing a little more mayonnaise along the upper edge of the row of potatoes where the next row overlaps will help the potato slices stick. Press the potatoes onto the fish to secure them well and season again with salt. Brush or spray the potato layer with olive oil.

3. Transfer the fish to the air fryer and air-fry for 8 to 10 minutes, depending on the thickness of your fillets. 1-inch of fish should take 10 minutes at 400°F.

4. While the fish is cooking, add the garlic, capers, olive oil and lemon juice to the remaining mayonnaise mixture to make the caper aïoli.

5. Serve the fish warm with a dollop of the aïoli on top or on the side.

Crab Cakes On A Budget

Servings: 4
Cooking Time: 12 Minutes

Ingredients:

* 8 ounces imitation crabmeat
* 4 ounces leftover cooked fish (such as cod, pollock, or haddock)
* 2 tablespoons minced green onion
* 2 tablespoons minced celery
* ¾ cup crushed saltine cracker crumbs
* 2 tablespoons light mayonnaise
* 1 teaspoon prepared yellow mustard
* 1 tablespoon Worcestershire sauce, plus 2 teaspoons
* 2 teaspoons dried parsley flakes
* ½ teaspoon dried dill weed, crushed
* ½ teaspoon garlic powder
* ½ teaspoon Old Bay Seasoning
* ½ cup panko breadcrumbs
* oil for misting or cooking spray

Directions:

1. Use knives or a food processor to finely shred crabmeat and fish.

2. In a large bowl, combine all ingredients except panko and oil. Stir well.

3. Shape into 8 small, fat patties.

4. Carefully roll patties in panko crumbs to coat. Spray both sides with oil or cooking spray.

5. Place patties in air fryer basket and cook at 390°F for 12 minutes or until golden brown and crispy.

Buttery Lobster Tails

Servings:4
Cooking Time: 6 Minutes

Ingredients:

* 4 6- to 8-ounce shell-on raw lobster tails
* 2 tablespoons Butter, melted and cooled
* 1 teaspoon Lemon juice
* ½ teaspoon Finely grated lemon zest
* ½ teaspoon Garlic powder
* ½ teaspoon Table salt
* ½ teaspoon Ground black pepper

Directions:

1. Preheat the air fryer to 375°F .

2. To give the tails that restaurant look, you need to butterfly the meat. To do so, place a tail on a cutting board so that the shell is convex. Use kitchen shears to cut a line down the middle of the shell from the larger end to the smaller, cutting only the shell and not the meat below, and stopping before the back fins. Pry open the shell, leaving it intact. Use your clean fingers to separate the meat from the shell's sides and bottom, keeping it attached to the shell at the back near the fins. Pull the meat up and out of the shell through the cut line, laying the meat on top of the shell and closing the shell (as well as you can) under the meat. Make two equidistant cuts down the meat from the larger end to near the smaller end, each about ¼ inch deep, for the classic restaurant look on the plate. Repeat this procedure with the remaining tail(s).

3. Stir the butter, lemon juice, zest, garlic powder, salt, and pepper in a small bowl until well combined. Brush this mixture over the lobster meat set atop the shells.

4. When the machine is at temperature, place the tails shell side down in the basket with as

much air space between them as possible. Air-fry undisturbed for 6 minutes, or until the lobster meat has pink streaks over it and is firm.

5. Use kitchen tongs to transfer the tails to a wire rack. Cool for only a minute or two before serving.

Firecracker Popcorn Shrimp

Servings: 6
Cooking Time: 8 Minutes

Ingredients:
- ½ cup all-purpose flour
- 2 teaspoons ground paprika
- 1 teaspoon garlic powder
- ½ teaspoon black pepper
- ¼ teaspoon salt
- 2 eggs, whisked
- 1½ cups panko breadcrumbs
- 1 pound small shrimp, peeled and deveined

Directions:
1. Preheat the air fryer to 360°F.
2. In a medium bowl, place the flour and mix in the paprika, garlic powder, pepper, and salt.
3. In a shallow dish, place the eggs.
4. In a third dish, place the breadcrumbs.
5. Assemble the shrimp by covering them in the flour, then dipping them into the egg, and then coating them with the breadcrumbs. Repeat until all the shrimp are covered in the breading.
6. Liberally spray the metal trivet that fits in the air fryer basket with olive oil mist. Place the shrimp onto the trivet, leaving space between the shrimp to flip. Cook for 4 minutes, flip the shrimp, and cook another 4 minutes. Repeat until all the shrimp are cooked.
7. Serve warm with desired dipping sauce.

Almond-crusted Fish

Servings: 4
Cooking Time: 10 Minutes

Ingredients:
- 4 4-ounce fish fillets
- ¾ cup breadcrumbs
- ¼ cup sliced almonds, crushed
- 2 tablespoons lemon juice
- ⅛ teaspoon cayenne
- salt and pepper
- ¾ cup flour
- 1 egg, beaten with 1 tablespoon water
- oil for misting or cooking spray

Directions:
1. Split fish fillets lengthwise down the center to create 8 pieces.
2. Mix breadcrumbs and almonds together and set aside.
3. Mix the lemon juice and cayenne together. Brush on all sides of fish.
4. Season fish to taste with salt and pepper.
5. Place the flour on a sheet of wax paper.
6. Roll fillets in flour, dip in egg wash, and roll in the crumb mixture.
7. Mist both sides of fish with oil or cooking spray.
8. Spray air fryer basket and lay fillets inside.
9. Cook at 390°F for 5minutes, turn fish over, and cook for an additional 5minutes or until fish is done and flakes easily.

Cajun Flounder Fillets

Servings:2

Cooking Time: 5 Minutes

Ingredients:

- 2 4-ounce skinless flounder fillet(s)
- 2 teaspoons Peanut oil
- 1 teaspoon Purchased or homemade Cajun dried seasoning blend (see the headnote)

Directions:

1. Preheat the air fryer to 400°F.
2. Oil the fillet(s) by drizzling on the peanut oil, then gently rubbing in the oil with your clean, dry fingers. Sprinkle the seasoning blend evenly over both sides of the fillet(s).
3. When the machine is at temperature, set the fillet(s) in the basket. If working with more than one fillet, they should not touch, although they may be quite close together, depending on the basket's size. Air-fry undisturbed for 5 minutes, or until lightly browned and cooked through.
4. Use a nonstick-safe spatula to transfer the fillets to a serving platter or plate(s). Serve at once.

Blackened Catfish

Servings: 4

Cooking Time: 8 Minutes

Ingredients:

- 1 teaspoon paprika
- 1 teaspoon garlic powder
- 1 teaspoon onion powder
- 1 teaspoon ground dried thyme
- ½ teaspoon ground black pepper
- ⅛ teaspoon cayenne pepper
- ½ teaspoon dried oregano
- ⅛ teaspoon crushed red pepper flakes
- 1 pound catfish filets

- ½ teaspoon sea salt
- 2 tablespoons butter, melted
- 1 tablespoon extra-virgin olive oil
- 2 tablespoons chopped parsley
- 1 lemon, cut into wedges

Directions:

1. In a small bowl, stir together the paprika, garlic powder, onion powder, thyme, black pepper, cayenne pepper, oregano, and crushed red pepper flakes.
2. Pat the fish dry with paper towels. Season the filets with sea salt and then coat with the blackening seasoning.
3. In a small bowl, mix together the butter and olive oil and drizzle over the fish filets, flipping them to coat them fully.
4. Preheat the air fryer to 350°F.
5. Place the fish in the air fryer basket and cook for 8 minutes, checking the fish for doneness after 4 minutes. The fish will flake easily when cooked.
6. Remove the fish from the air fryer. Top with chopped parsley and serve with lemon wedges.

Miso-rubbed Salmon Fillets

Servings:3

Cooking Time: 5 Minutes

Ingredients:

- ¼ cup White (shiro) miso paste (usually made from rice and soy beans)
- 1½ tablespoons Mirin or a substitute (see here)
- 2½ teaspoons Unseasoned rice vinegar (see here)
- Vegetable oil spray
- 3 6-ounce skin-on salmon fillets (for more information, see here)

Directions:

1. Preheat the air fryer to 400°F.

2. Mix the miso, mirin, and vinegar in a small bowl until uniform.

3. Remove the basket from the machine. Generously spray the skin side of each fillet. Pick them up one by one with a nonstick-safe spatula and set them in the basket skin side down with as much air space between them as possible. Coat the top of each fillet with the miso mixture, dividing it evenly between them.

4. Return the basket to the machine. Air-fry undisturbed for 5 minutes, or until lightly browned and firm.

5. Use a nonstick-safe spatula to transfer the fillets to serving plates. Cool for only a minute or so before serving.

Catfish Nuggets

Servings: 4
Cooking Time: 7 Minutes Per Batch

Ingredients:
- 2 medium catfish fillets, cut in chunks (approximately 1 x 2 inch)
- salt and pepper
- 2 eggs
- 2 tablespoons skim milk
- ½ cup cornstarch
- 1 cup panko breadcrumbs, crushed
- oil for misting or cooking spray

Directions:
1. Season catfish chunks with salt and pepper to your liking.
2. Beat together eggs and milk in a small bowl.
3. Place cornstarch in a second small bowl.
4. Place breadcrumbs in a third small bowl.
5. Dip catfish chunks in cornstarch, dip in egg wash, shake off excess, then roll in breadcrumbs.
6. Spray all sides of catfish chunks with oil or cooking spray.

7. Place chunks in air fryer basket in a single layer, leaving space between for air circulation.
8. Cook at 390°F for 4minutes, turn, and cook an additional 3 minutes, until fish flakes easily and outside is crispy brown.
9. Repeat steps 7 and 8 to cook remaining catfish nuggets.

Maple-crusted Salmon

Servings: 2
Cooking Time: 8 Minutes

Ingredients:
- 12 ounces salmon filets
- ⅓ cup maple syrup
- 1 teaspoon Worcestershire sauce
- 2 teaspoons Dijon mustard or brown mustard
- ½ cup finely chopped walnuts
- ½ teaspoon sea salt
- ½ lemon
- 1 tablespoon chopped parsley, for garnish

Directions:
1. Place the salmon in a shallow baking dish. Top with maple syrup, Worcestershire sauce, and mustard. Refrigerate for 30 minutes.
2. Preheat the air fryer to 350°F.
3. Remove the salmon from the marinade and discard the marinade.
4. Place the chopped nuts on top of the salmon filets, and sprinkle salt on top of the nuts. Place the salmon, skin side down, in the air fryer basket. Cook for 6 to 8 minutes or until the fish flakes in the center.
5. Remove the salmon and plate on a serving platter. Squeeze fresh lemon over the top of the salmon and top with chopped parsley. Serve immediately.

Perfect Soft-shelled Crabs

Servings:2

Cooking Time: 12 Minutes

Ingredients:

- ½ cup All-purpose flour
- 1 tablespoon Old Bay seasoning
- 1 Large egg(s), well beaten
- 1 cup (about 3 ounces) Ground oyster crackers
- 2 2½-ounce cleaned soft-shelled crab(s), about 4 inches across
- Vegetable oil spray

Directions:

1. Preheat the air fryer to 375°F (or 380°F or 390°F, if one of these is the closest setting).

2. Set up and fill three shallow soup plates or small pie plates on your counter: one for the flour, whisked with the Old Bay until well combined; one for the beaten egg(s); and one for the cracker crumbs.

3. Set a soft-shelled crab in the flour mixture and turn to coat evenly and well on all sides, even inside the legs. Dip the crab into the egg(s) and coat well, turning at least once, again getting some of the egg between the legs. Let any excess egg slip back into the rest, then set the crab in the cracker crumbs. Turn several times, pressing very gently to get the crab evenly coated with crumbs, even between the legs. Generously coat the crab on all sides with vegetable oil spray. Set it aside if you're making more than one and coat these in the same way.

4. Set the crab(s) in the basket with as much air space between them as possible. They may overlap slightly, particularly at the ends of their legs, depending on the basket's size. Air-fry undisturbed for 12 minutes, or until very crisp and golden brown. If the machine is at 390°F, the crabs may be done in only 10 minutes.

5. Use kitchen tongs to gently transfer the crab(s) to a wire rack. Cool for a couple of minutes before serving.

Tilapia Teriyaki

Servings: 3
Cooking Time: 10 Minutes

Ingredients:

- 4 tablespoons teriyaki sauce
- 1 tablespoon pineapple juice
- 1 pound tilapia fillets
- cooking spray
- 6 ounces frozen mixed peppers with onions, thawed and drained
- 2 cups cooked rice

Directions:

1. Mix the teriyaki sauce and pineapple juice together in a small bowl.

2. Split tilapia fillets down the center lengthwise.

3. Brush all sides of fish with the sauce, spray air fryer basket with nonstick cooking spray, and place fish in the basket.

4. Stir the peppers and onions into the remaining sauce and spoon over the fish. Save any leftover sauce for drizzling over the fish when serving.

5. Cook at 360°F for 10 minutes, until fish flakes easily with a fork and is done in center.

6. Divide into 3 or 4 servings and serve each with approximately ½ cup cooked rice.

Shrimp

Servings: 4

Cooking Time: 8 Minutes

Ingredients:

- 1 pound (26–30 count) shrimp, peeled, deveined, and butterflied (last tail section of shell intact)
- Marinade
- 1 5-ounce can evaporated milk
- 2 eggs, beaten
- 2 tablespoons white vinegar
- 1 tablespoon baking powder
- Coating
- 1 cup crushed panko breadcrumbs
- ½ teaspoon paprika
- ½ teaspoon Old Bay Seasoning
- ¼ teaspoon garlic powder
- oil for misting or cooking spray

Directions:

1. Stir together all marinade ingredients until well mixed. Add shrimp and stir to coat. Refrigerate for 1 hour.

2. When ready to cook, preheat air fryer to 390°F.

3. Combine coating ingredients in shallow dish.

4. Remove shrimp from marinade, roll in crumb mixture, and spray with olive oil or cooking spray.

5. Cooking in two batches, place shrimp in air fryer basket in single layer, close but not overlapping. Cook at 390°F for 8 minutes, until light golden brown and crispy.

6. Repeat step 5 to cook remaining shrimp.

Shrimp Teriyaki

Servings:10

Cooking Time: 6 Minutes

Ingredients:

- 1 tablespoon Regular or low-sodium soy sauce or gluten-free tamari sauce
- 1 tablespoon Mirin or a substitute (see here)
- 1 teaspoon Ginger juice (see the headnote)
- 10 Large shrimp (20–25 per pound), peeled and deveined
- ⅔ cup Plain panko bread crumbs (gluten-free, if a concern)
- 1 Large egg
- Vegetable oil spray

Directions:

1. Whisk the soy or tamari sauce, mirin, and ginger juice in an 8- or 9-inch square baking pan until uniform. Add the shrimp and toss well to coat. Cover and refrigerate for 1 hour, tossing the shrimp in the marinade at least twice.

2. Preheat the air fryer to 400°F.

3. Thread a marinated shrimp on a 4-inch bamboo skewer by inserting the pointy tip at the small end of the shrimp, then guiding the skewer along the shrimp so that the tip comes out the thick end and the shrimp is flat along the length of the skewer. Repeat with the remaining shrimp. (You'll need eight 4-inch skewers for the small batch, 10 skewers for the medium batch, and 12 for the large.)

4. Pour the bread crumbs onto a dinner plate. Whisk the egg in the baking pan with any marinade that stayed behind. Lay the skewers in the pan, in as close to a single layer as possible. Turn repeatedly to make sure the shrimp is coated in the egg mixture.

5. One at a time, take a skewered shrimp out of the pan and set it in the bread crumbs, turning several times and pressing gently until the shrimp is evenly coated on all sides. Coat the shrimp with

vegetable oil spray and set the skewer aside. Repeat with the remainder of the shrimp.

6. Set the skewered shrimp in the basket in one layer. Air-fry undisturbed for 6 minutes, or until pink and firm.

7. Transfer the skewers to a wire rack. Cool for only a minute or two before serving.

Salmon Puttanesca En Papillotte With Zucchini

Servings: 2

Cooking Time: 17 Minutes

Ingredients:
- 1 small zucchini, sliced into ¼-inch thick half moons
- 1 teaspoon olive oil
- salt and freshly ground black pepper
- 2 (5-ounce) salmon fillets
- 1 beefsteak tomato, chopped (about 1 cup)
- 1 tablespoon capers, rinsed
- 10 black olives, pitted and sliced
- 2 tablespoons dry vermouth or white wine 2 tablespoons butter
- ¼ cup chopped fresh basil, chopped

Directions:
1. Preheat the air fryer to 400°F.
2. Toss the zucchini with the olive oil, salt and freshly ground black pepper. Transfer the zucchini into the air fryer basket and air-fry for 5 minutes, shaking the basket once or twice during the cooking process.
3. Cut out 2 large rectangles of parchment paper – about 13-inches by 15-inches each. Divide the air-fried zucchini between the two pieces of parchment paper, placing the vegetables in the center of each rectangle.

4. Place a fillet of salmon on each pile of zucchini. Season the fish very well with salt and pepper. Toss the tomato, capers, olives and vermouth (or white wine) together in a bowl. Divide the tomato mixture between the two fish packages, placing it on top of the fish fillets and pouring any juice out of the bowl onto the fish. Top each fillet with a tablespoon of butter.

5. Fold up each parchment square. Bring two edges together and fold them over a few times, leaving some space above the fish. Twist the open sides together and upwards so they can serve as handles for the packet, but don't let them extend beyond the top of the air fryer basket.

6. Place the two packages into the air fryer and air-fry at 400°F for 12 minutes. The packages should be puffed up and slightly browned when fully cooked. Once cooked, let the fish sit in the parchment for 2 minutes.

7. Serve the fish in the parchment paper, or if desired, remove the parchment paper before serving. Garnish with a little fresh basil.

Shrimp Po'boy With Remoulade Sauce

Servings: 6

Cooking Time: 8 Minutes

Ingredients:
- ½ cup all-purpose flour
- ½ teaspoon paprika
- 1 teaspoon garlic powder
- ½ teaspoon black pepper
- ¼ teaspoon salt
- 2 eggs, whisked
- 1½ cups panko breadcrumbs
- 1 pound small shrimp, peeled and deveined
- Six 6-inch French rolls

- 2 cups shredded lettuce
- 12 ⅛-inch tomato slices
- ¾ cup Remoulade Sauce (see the following recipe)

Directions:

1. Preheat the air fryer to 360°F.
2. In a medium bowl, mix the flour, paprika, garlic powder, pepper, and salt.
3. In a shallow dish, place the eggs.
4. In a third dish, place the panko breadcrumbs.
5. Covering the shrimp in the flour, dip them into the egg, and coat them with the breadcrumbs. Repeat until all shrimp are covered in the breading.
6. Liberally spray the metal trivet that fits inside the air fryer basket with olive oil spray. Place the shrimp onto the trivet, leaving space between the shrimp to flip. Cook for 4 minutes, flip the shrimp, and cook another 4 minutes. Repeat until all the shrimp are cooked.
7. Slice the rolls in half. Stuff each roll with shredded lettuce, tomato slices, breaded shrimp, and remoulade sauce. Serve immediately.

Crunchy Clam Strips

Servings:3
Cooking Time: 8 Minutes

Ingredients:

- ½ pound Clam strips, drained
- 1 Large egg, well beaten
- ½ cup All-purpose flour
- ½ cup Yellow cornmeal
- 1½ teaspoons Table salt
- 1½ teaspoons Ground black pepper
- Up to ¾ teaspoon Cayenne
- Vegetable oil spray

Directions:

1. Preheat the air fryer to 400°F.
2. Toss the clam strips and beaten egg in a bowl until the clams are well coated.
3. Mix the flour, cornmeal, salt, pepper, and cayenne in a large zip-closed plastic bag until well combined. Using a flatware fork or small kitchen tongs, lift the clam strips one by one out of the egg, letting any excess egg slip back into the rest. Put the strips in the bag with the flour mixture. Once all the strips are in the bag, seal it and shake gently until the strips are well coated.
4. Use kitchen tongs to pick out the clam strips and lay them on a cutting board (leaving any extra flour mixture in the bag to be discarded). Coat the strips on both sides with vegetable oil spray.
5. When the machine is at temperature, spread the clam strips in the basket in one layer. They may touch in places, but try to leave as much air space as possible around them. Air-fry undisturbed for 8 minutes, or until brown and crunchy.
6. Gently dump the contents of the basket onto a serving platter. Cool for just a minute or two before serving hot.

SANDWICHES AND BURGERS RECIPES

Eggplant Parmesan Subs

Servings: 2
Cooking Time: 13 Minutes

Ingredients:

- 4 Peeled eggplant slices (about ½ inch thick and 3 inches in diameter)
- Olive oil spray
- 2 tablespoons plus 2 teaspoons Jarred pizza sauce, any variety except creamy
- ¼ cup (about ⅔ ounce) Finely grated Parmesan cheese
- 2 Small, long soft rolls, such as hero, hoagie, or Italian sub rolls (gluten-free, if a concern), split open lengthwise

Directions:

1. Preheat the air fryer to 350°F .

2. When the machine is at temperature, coat both sides of the eggplant slices with olive oil spray. Set them in the basket in one layer and air-fry undisturbed for 10 minutes, until lightly browned and softened.

3. Increase the machine's temperature to 375°F (or 370°F, if that's the closest setting—unless the machine is already at 360°F, in which case leave it alone). Top each eggplant slice with 2 teaspoons pizza sauce, then 1 tablespoon cheese. Air-fry undisturbed for 2 minutes, or until the cheese has melted.

4. Use a nonstick-safe spatula, and perhaps a flatware fork for balance, to transfer the eggplant slices cheese side up to a cutting board. Set the roll(s) cut side down in the basket in one layer (working in batches as necessary) and air-fry undisturbed for 1 minute, to toast the rolls a bit and warm them up. Set 2 eggplant slices in each warm roll.

Lamb Burgers

Servings: 3
Cooking Time: 17 Minutes

Ingredients:

- 1 pound 2 ounces Ground lamb
- 3 tablespoons Crumbled feta
- 1 teaspoon Minced garlic
- 1 teaspoon Tomato paste
- ¾ teaspoon Ground coriander
- ¾ teaspoon Ground dried ginger
- Up to ⅛ teaspoon Cayenne
- Up to a ⅛ teaspoon Table salt (optional)
- 3 Kaiser rolls or hamburger buns (gluten-free, if a concern), split open

Directions:

1. Preheat the air fryer to 375°F .

2. Gently mix the ground lamb, feta, garlic, tomato paste, coriander, ginger, cayenne, and salt (if using) in a bowl until well combined, trying to keep the bits of cheese intact. Form this mixture into two 5-inch patties for the small batch, three 5-inch patties for the medium, or four 5-inch patties for the large.

3. Set the patties in the basket in one layer and air-fry undisturbed for 16 minutes, or until an instant-read meat thermometer inserted into one burger registers 160°F. (The cheese is not an issue with the temperature probe in this recipe as it was for the Inside-Out Cheeseburgers, because the feta is so well mixed into the ground meat.)

4. Use a nonstick-safe spatula, and perhaps a flatware fork for balance, to transfer the burgers

to a cutting board. Set the buns cut side down in the basket in one layer (working in batches as necessary) and air-fry undisturbed for 1 minute, to toast a bit and warm up. Serve the burgers warm in the buns.

Sausage And Pepper Heros

Servings: 3
Cooking Time: 11 Minutes

Ingredients:

- 3 links (about 9 ounces total) Sweet Italian sausages (gluten-free, if a concern)
- 1½ Medium red or green bell pepper(s), stemmed, cored, and cut into ½-inch-wide strips
- 1 medium Yellow or white onion(s), peeled, halved, and sliced into thin half-moons
- 3 Long soft rolls, such as hero, hoagie, or Italian sub rolls (gluten-free, if a concern), split open lengthwise
- For garnishing Balsamic vinegar
- For garnishing Fresh basil leaves

Directions:

1. Preheat the air fryer to 400°F.

2. When the machine is at temperature, set the sausage links in the basket in one layer and air-fry undisturbed for 5 minutes.

3. Add the pepper strips and onions. Continue air-frying, tossing and rearranging everything about once every minute, for 5 minutes, or until the sausages are browned and an instant-read meat thermometer inserted into one of the links registers 160°F.

4. Use a nonstick-safe spatula and kitchen tongs to transfer the sausages and vegetables to a cutting board. Set the rolls cut side down in the basket in one layer (working in batches as necessary) and air-fry undisturbed for 1 minute,

to toast the rolls a bit and warm them up. Set 1 sausage with some pepper strips and onions in each warm roll, sprinkle balsamic vinegar over the sandwich fillings, and garnish with basil leaves.

Chicken Gyros

Servings: 4
Cooking Time: 14 Minutes

Ingredients:

- 4 4- to 5-ounce boneless skinless chicken thighs, trimmed of any fat blobs
- 2 tablespoons Lemon juice
- 2 tablespoons Red wine vinegar
- 2 tablespoons Olive oil
- 2 teaspoons Dried oregano
- 2 teaspoons Minced garlic
- 1 teaspoon Table salt
- 1 teaspoon Ground black pepper
- 4 Pita pockets (gluten-free, if a concern)
- ½ cup Chopped tomatoes
- ½ cup Bottled regular, low-fat, or fat-free ranch dressing (gluten-free, if a concern)

Directions:

1. Mix the thighs, lemon juice, vinegar, oil, oregano, garlic, salt, and pepper in a zip-closed bag. Seal, gently massage the marinade into the meat through the plastic, and refrigerate for at least 2 hours or up to 6 hours. (Longer than that and the meat can turn rubbery.)

2. Set the plastic bag out on the counter (to make the contents a little less frigid). Preheat the air fryer to 375°F .

3. When the machine is at temperature, use kitchen tongs to place the thighs in the basket in one layer. Discard the marinade. Air-fry the chicken thighs undisturbed for 12 minutes, or until browned and an instant-read meat

thermometer inserted into the thickest part of one thigh registers 165°F. You may need to air-fry the chicken 2 minutes longer if the machine's temperature is 360°F.

4. Use kitchen tongs to transfer the thighs to a cutting board. Cool for 5 minutes, then set one thigh in each of the pita pockets. Top each with 2 tablespoons chopped tomatoes and 2 tablespoons dressing. Serve warm.

Dijon Thyme Burgers

Servings: 3
Cooking Time: 18 Minutes

Ingredients:

- 1 pound lean ground beef
- ⅓ cup panko breadcrumbs
- ¼ cup finely chopped onion
- 3 tablespoons Dijon mustard
- 1 tablespoon chopped fresh thyme
- 4 teaspoons Worcestershire sauce
- 1 teaspoon salt
- freshly ground black pepper
- Topping (optional):
- 2 tablespoons Dijon mustard
- 1 tablespoon dark brown sugar
- 1 teaspoon Worcestershire sauce
- 4 ounces sliced Swiss cheese, optional

Directions:

1. Combine all the burger ingredients together in a large bowl and mix well. Divide the meat into 4 equal portions and then form the burgers, being careful not to over-handle the meat. One good way to do this is to throw the meat back and forth from one hand to another, packing the meat each time you catch it. Flatten the balls into patties, making an indentation in the center of each patty with your thumb (this will help it stay flat as it cooks) and flattening the sides of the burgers so that they will fit nicely into the air fryer basket.

2. Preheat the air fryer to 370°F.

3. If you don't have room for all four burgers, air-fry two or three burgers at a time for 8 minutes. Flip the burgers over and air-fry for another 6 minutes.

4. While the burgers are cooking combine the Dijon mustard, dark brown sugar, and Worcestershire sauce in a small bowl and mix well. This optional topping to the burgers really adds a boost of flavor at the end. Spread the Dijon topping evenly on each burger. If you cooked the burgers in batches, return the first batch to the cooker at this time – it's ok to place the fourth burger on top of the others in the center of the basket. Air-fry the burgers for another 3 minutes.

5. Finally, if desired, top each burger with a slice of Swiss cheese. Lower the air fryer temperature to 330°F and air-fry for another minute to melt the cheese. Serve the burgers on toasted brioche buns, dressed the way you like them.

Crunchy Falafel Balls

Servings: 8
Cooking Time: 16 Minutes

Ingredients:

- 2½ cups Drained and rinsed canned chickpeas
- ¼ cup Olive oil
- 3 tablespoons All-purpose flour
- 1½ teaspoons Dried oregano
- 1½ teaspoons Dried sage leaves
- 1½ teaspoons Dried thyme
- ¾ teaspoon Table salt
- Olive oil spray

Directions:

1. Preheat the air fryer to 400°F.

2. Place the chickpeas, olive oil, flour, oregano, sage, thyme, and salt in a food processor. Cover and process into a paste, stopping the machine at least once to scrape down the inside of the canister.

3. Scrape down and remove the blade. Using clean, wet hands, form 2 tablespoons of the paste into a ball, then continue making 9 more balls for a small batch, 15 more for a medium one, and 19 more for a large batch. Generously coat the balls in olive oil spray.

4. Set the balls in the basket in one layer with a little space between them and air-fry undisturbed for 16 minutes, or until well browned and crisp.

5. Dump the contents of the basket onto a wire rack. Cool for 5 minutes before serving.

Provolone Stuffed Meatballs

Servings: 4
Cooking Time: 12 Minutes

Ingredients:

- 1 tablespoon olive oil
- 1 small onion, very finely chopped
- 1 to 2 cloves garlic, minced
- ¾ pound ground beef
- ¾ pound ground pork
- ¾ cup breadcrumbs
- ¼ cup grated Parmesan cheese
- ¼ cup finely chopped fresh parsley (or 1 tablespoon dried parsley)
- ½ teaspoon dried oregano
- 1½ teaspoons salt
- freshly ground black pepper
- 2 eggs, lightly beaten
- 5 ounces sharp or aged provolone cheese, cut into 1-inch cubes

Directions:

1. Preheat a skillet over medium-high heat. Add the oil and cook the onion and garlic until tender, but not browned.

2. Transfer the onion and garlic to a large bowl and add the beef, pork, breadcrumbs, Parmesan cheese, parsley, oregano, salt, pepper and eggs. Mix well until all the ingredients are combined. Divide the mixture into 12 evenly sized balls. Make one meatball at a time, by pressing a hole in the meatball mixture with your finger and pushing a piece of provolone cheese into the hole. Mold the meat back into a ball, enclosing the cheese.

3. Preheat the air fryer to 380°F.

4. Working in two batches, transfer six of the meatballs to the air fryer basket and air-fry for 12 minutes, shaking the basket and turning the meatballs a couple of times during the cooking process. Repeat with the remaining six meatballs. You can pop the first batch of meatballs into the air fryer for the last two minutes of cooking to reheat them. Serve warm.

Thanksgiving Turkey Sandwiches

Servings: 3
Cooking Time: 10 Minutes

Ingredients:

- 1½ cups Herb-seasoned stuffing mix (not cornbread-style; gluten-free, if a concern)
- 1 Large egg white(s)
- 2 tablespoons Water
- 3 5- to 6-ounce turkey breast cutlets
- Vegetable oil spray
- 4½ tablespoons Purchased cranberry sauce, preferably whole berry

- ⅛ teaspoon Ground cinnamon
- ⅛ teaspoon Ground dried ginger
- 4½ tablespoons Regular, low-fat, or fat-free mayonnaise (gluten-free, if a concern)
- 6 tablespoons Shredded Brussels sprouts
- 3 Kaiser rolls (gluten-free, if a concern), split open

Directions:

1. Preheat the air fryer to 375°F .
2. Put the stuffing mix in a heavy zip-closed bag, seal it, lay it flat on your counter, and roll a rolling pin over the bag to crush the stuffing mix to the consistency of rough sand. (Or you can pulse the stuffing mix to the desired consistency in a food processor.)
3. Set up and fill two shallow soup plates or small pie plates on your counter: one for the egg white(s), whisked with the water until foamy; and one for the ground stuffing mix.
4. Dip a cutlet in the egg white mixture, coating both sides and letting any excess egg white slip back into the rest. Set the cutlet in the ground stuffing mix and coat it evenly on both sides, pressing gently to coat well on both sides. Lightly coat the cutlet on both sides with vegetable oil spray, set it aside, and continue dipping and coating the remaining cutlets in the same way.
5. Set the cutlets in the basket and air-fry undisturbed for 10 minutes, or until crisp and brown. Use kitchen tongs to transfer the cutlets to a wire rack to cool for a few minutes.
6. Meanwhile, stir the cranberry sauce with the cinnamon and ginger in a small bowl. Mix the shredded Brussels sprouts and mayonnaise in a second bowl until the vegetable is evenly coated.
7. Build the sandwiches by spreading about 1½ tablespoons of the cranberry mixture on the cut side of the bottom half of each roll. Set a cutlet on top, then spread about 3 tablespoons of the Brussels sprouts mixture evenly over the cutlet. Set the other half of the roll on top and serve warm.

Philly Cheesesteak Sandwiches

Servings: 3
Cooking Time: 9 Minutes

Ingredients:

- ¾ pound Shaved beef
- 1 tablespoon Worcestershire sauce (gluten-free, if a concern)
- ¼ teaspoon Garlic powder
- ¼ teaspoon Mild paprika
- 6 tablespoons (1½ ounces) Frozen bell pepper strips (do not thaw)
- 2 slices, broken into rings Very thin yellow or white medium onion slice(s)
- 6 ounces (6 to 8 slices) Provolone cheese slices
- 3 Long soft rolls such as hero, hoagie, or Italian sub rolls, or hot dog buns (gluten-free, if a concern), split open lengthwise

Directions:

1. Preheat the air fryer to 400°F.
2. When the machine is at temperature, spread the shaved beef in the basket, leaving a ½-inch perimeter around the meat for good air flow. Sprinkle the meat with the Worcestershire sauce, paprika, and garlic powder. Spread the peppers and onions on top of the meat.
3. Air-fry undisturbed for 6 minutes, or until cooked through. Set the cheese on top of the meat. Continue air-frying undisturbed for 3 minutes, or until the cheese has melted.
4. Use kitchen tongs to divide the meat and cheese layers in the basket between the rolls or buns. Serve hot.

Chicken Club Sandwiches

Servings: 3

Cooking Time: 15 Minutes

Ingredients:

- 3 5- to 6-ounce boneless skinless chicken breasts
- 6 Thick-cut bacon strips (gluten-free, if a concern)
- 3 Long soft rolls, such as hero, hoagie, or Italian sub rolls (gluten-free, if a concern)
- 3 tablespoons Regular, low-fat, or fat-free mayonnaise (gluten-free, if a concern)
- 3 Lettuce leaves, preferably romaine or iceberg
- 6 ¼-inch-thick tomato slices

Directions:

1. Preheat the air fryer to 375°F .

2. Wrap each chicken breast with 2 strips of bacon, spiraling the bacon around the meat, slightly overlapping the strips on each revolution. Start the second strip of bacon farther down the breast but on a line with the start of the first strip so they both end at a lined-up point on the chicken breast.

3. When the machine is at temperature, set the wrapped breasts bacon-seam side down in the basket with space between them. Air-fry undisturbed for 12 minutes, until the bacon is browned, crisp, and cooked through and an instant-read meat thermometer inserted into the center of a breast registers 165°F. You may need to add 2 minutes in the air fryer if the temperature is at 360°F.

4. Use kitchen tongs to transfer the breasts to a wire rack. Split the rolls open lengthwise and set them cut side down in the basket. Air-fry for 1 minute, or until warmed through.

5. Use kitchen tongs to transfer the rolls to a cutting board. Spread 1 tablespoon mayonnaise on the cut side of one half of each roll. Top with a chicken breast, lettuce leaf, and tomato slice. Serve warm.

Chicken Saltimbocca Sandwiches

Servings: 3

Cooking Time: 11 Minutes

Ingredients:

- 3 5- to 6-ounce boneless skinless chicken breasts
- 6 Thin prosciutto slices
- 6 Provolone cheese slices
- 3 Long soft rolls, such as hero, hoagie, or Italian sub rolls (gluten-free, if a concern), split open lengthwise
- 3 tablespoons Pesto, purchased or homemade (see the headnote)

Directions:

1. Preheat the air fryer to 400°F.

2. Wrap each chicken breast with 2 prosciutto slices, spiraling the prosciutto around the breast and overlapping the slices a bit to cover the breast. The prosciutto will stick to the chicken more readily than bacon does.

3. When the machine is at temperature, set the wrapped chicken breasts in the basket and air-fry undisturbed for 10 minutes, or until the prosciutto is frizzled and the chicken is cooked through.

4. Overlap 2 cheese slices on each breast. Air-fry undisturbed for 1 minute, or until melted. Take the basket out of the machine.

5. Smear the insides of the rolls with the pesto, then use kitchen tongs to put a wrapped and cheesy chicken breast in each roll.

Chili Cheese Dogs

Servings: 3

Cooking Time: 12 Minutes

Ingredients:

- ¾ pound Lean ground beef
- 1½ tablespoons Chile powder
- 1 cup plus 2 tablespoons Jarred sofrito
- 3 Hot dogs (gluten-free, if a concern)
- 3 Hot dog buns (gluten-free, if a concern), split open lengthwise
- 3 tablespoons Finely chopped scallion
- 9 tablespoons (a little more than 2 ounces) Shredded Cheddar cheese

Directions:

1. Crumble the ground beef into a medium or large saucepan set over medium heat. Brown well, stirring often to break up the clumps. Add the chile powder and cook for 30 seconds, stirring the whole time. Stir in the sofrito and bring to a simmer. Reduce the heat to low and simmer, stirring occasionally, for 5 minutes. Keep warm.

2. Preheat the air fryer to 400°F.

3. When the machine is at temperature, put the hot dogs in the basket and air-fry undisturbed for 10 minutes, or until the hot dogs are bubbling and blistered, even a little crisp.

4. Use kitchen tongs to put the hot dogs in the buns. Top each with a ½ cup of the ground beef mixture, 1 tablespoon of the minced scallion, and 3 tablespoons of the cheese. (The scallion should go under the cheese so it superheats and wilts a bit.) Set the filled hot dog buns in the basket and air-fry undisturbed for 2 minutes, or until the cheese has melted.

5. Remove the basket from the machine. Cool the chili cheese dogs in the basket for 5 minutes before serving.

Black Bean Veggie Burgers

Servings: 3

Cooking Time: 10 Minutes

Ingredients:

- 1 cup Drained and rinsed canned black beans
- ⅓ cup Pecan pieces
- ⅓ cup Rolled oats (not quick-cooking or steel-cut; gluten-free, if a concern)
- 2 tablespoons (or 1 small egg) Pasteurized egg substitute, such as Egg Beaters (gluten-free, if a concern)
- 2 teaspoons Red ketchup-like chili sauce, such as Heinz
- ¼ teaspoon Ground cumin
- ¼ teaspoon Dried oregano
- ¼ teaspoon Table salt
- ¼ teaspoon Ground black pepper
- Olive oil
- Olive oil spray

Directions:

1. Preheat the air fryer to 400°F.

2. Put the beans, pecans, oats, egg substitute or egg, chili sauce, cumin, oregano, salt, and pepper in a food processor. Cover and process to a coarse paste that will hold its shape like sugar-cookie dough, adding olive oil in 1-teaspoon increments to get the mixture to blend smoothly. The amount of olive oil is actually dependent on the internal moisture content of the beans and the oats. Figure on about 1 tablespoon (three 1-teaspoon additions) for the smaller batch, with proportional increases for the other batches. A little too much olive oil can't hurt, but a dry paste will fall apart as it cooks and a far-too-wet paste will stick to the basket.

3. Scrape down and remove the blade. Using clean, wet hands, form the paste into two 4-inch

patties for the small batch, three 4-inch patties for the medium, or four 4-inch patties for the large batch, setting them one by one on a cutting board. Generously coat both sides of the patties with olive oil spray.

4. Set them in the basket in one layer. Air-fry undisturbed for 10 minutes, or until lightly browned and crisp at the edges.

5. Use a nonstick-safe spatula, and perhaps a flatware fork for balance, to transfer the burgers to a wire rack. Cool for 5 minutes before serving.

Best-ever Roast Beef Sandwiches

Servings: 6
Cooking Time: 30-50 Minutes

Ingredients:
- 2½ teaspoons Olive oil
- 1½ teaspoons Dried oregano
- 1½ teaspoons Dried thyme
- 1½ teaspoons Onion powder
- 1½ teaspoons Table salt
- 1½ teaspoons Ground black pepper
- 3 pounds Beef eye of round
- 6 Round soft rolls, such as Kaiser rolls or hamburger buns (gluten-free, if a concern), split open lengthwise
- ¾ cup Regular, low-fat, or fat-free mayonnaise (gluten-free, if a concern)
- 6 Romaine lettuce leaves, rinsed
- 6 Round tomato slices (¼ inch thick)

Directions:
1. Preheat the air fryer to 350°F .
2. Mix the oil, oregano, thyme, onion powder, salt, and pepper in a small bowl. Spread this mixture all over the eye of round.
3. When the machine is at temperature, set the beef in the basket and air-fry for 30 to 50 minutes (the range depends on the size of the cut), turning the meat twice, until an instant-read meat thermometer inserted into the thickest piece of the meat registers 130°F for rare, 140°F for medium, or 150°F for well-done.

4. Use kitchen tongs to transfer the beef to a cutting board. Cool for 10 minutes. If serving now, carve into ⅛-inch-thick slices. Spread each roll with 2 tablespoons mayonnaise and divide the beef slices between the rolls. Top with a lettuce leaf and a tomato slice and serve. Or set the beef in a container, cover, and refrigerate for up to 3 days to make cold roast beef sandwiches anytime.

Thai-style Pork Sliders

Servings: 4
Cooking Time: 15 Minutes

Ingredients:
- 11 ounces Ground pork
- 2½ tablespoons Very thinly sliced scallions, white and green parts
- 4 teaspoons Minced peeled fresh ginger
- 2½ teaspoons Fish sauce (gluten-free, if a concern)
- 2 teaspoons Thai curry paste (see the headnote; gluten-free, if a concern)
- 2 teaspoons Light brown sugar
- ¾ teaspoon Ground black pepper
- 4 Slider buns (gluten-free, if a concern)

Directions:
1. Preheat the air fryer to 375°F .
2. Gently mix the pork, scallions, ginger, fish sauce, curry paste, brown sugar, and black pepper in a bowl until well combined. With clean, wet hands, form about ⅓ cup of the pork mixture into a slider about 2½ inches in diameter. Repeat until you use up all the meat—3 sliders for the small

batch, 4 for the medium, and 6 for the large. (Keep wetting your hands to help the patties adhere.)

3. When the machine is at temperature, set the sliders in the basket in one layer. Air-fry undisturbed for 14 minutes, or until the sliders are golden brown and caramelized at their edges and an instant-read meat thermometer inserted into the center of a slider registers 160°F.

4. Use a nonstick-safe spatula, and perhaps a flatware fork for balance, to transfer the sliders to a cutting board. Set the buns cut side down in the basket in one layer (working in batches as necessary) and air-fry undisturbed for 1 minute, to toast a bit and warm up. Serve the sliders warm in the buns.

White Bean Veggie Burgers

Servings: 3
Cooking Time: 13 Minutes

Ingredients:

- 1⅓ cups Drained and rinsed canned white beans
- 3 tablespoons Rolled oats (not quick-cooking or steel-cut; gluten-free, if a concern)
- 3 tablespoons Chopped walnuts
- 2 teaspoons Olive oil
- 2 teaspoons Lemon juice
- 1½ teaspoons Dijon mustard (gluten-free, if a concern)
- ¾ teaspoon Dried sage leaves
- ¼ teaspoon Table salt
- Olive oil spray
- 3 Whole-wheat buns or gluten-free whole-grain buns (if a concern), split open

Directions:

1. Preheat the air fryer to 400°F.

2. Place the beans, oats, walnuts, oil, lemon juice, mustard, sage, and salt in a food processor. Cover and process to make a coarse paste that will hold its shape, about like wet sugar-cookie dough, stopping the machine to scrape down the inside of the canister at least once.

3. Scrape down and remove the blade. With clean and wet hands, form the bean paste into two 4-inch patties for the small batch, three 4-inch patties for the medium, or four 4-inch patties for the large batch. Generously coat the patties on both sides with olive oil spray.

4. Set them in the basket with some space between them and air-fry undisturbed for 12 minutes, or until lightly brown and crisp at the edges. The tops of the burgers will feel firm to the touch.

5. Use a nonstick-safe spatula, and perhaps a flatware fork for balance, to transfer the burgers to a cutting board. Set the buns cut side down in the basket in one layer (working in batches as necessary) and air-fry undisturbed for 1 minute, to toast a bit and warm up. Serve the burgers warm in the buns.

Chicken Apple Brie Melt

Servings: 3
Cooking Time: 13 Minutes

Ingredients:

- 3 5- to 6-ounce boneless skinless chicken breasts
- Vegetable oil spray
- 1½ teaspoons Dried herbes de Provence
- 3 ounces Brie, rind removed, thinly sliced
- 6 Thin cored apple slices
- 3 French rolls (gluten-free, if a concern)

- 2 tablespoons Dijon mustard (gluten-free, if a concern)

Directions:

1. Preheat the air fryer to 375°F .
2. Lightly coat all sides of the chicken breasts with vegetable oil spray. Sprinkle the breasts evenly with the herbes de Provence.
3. When the machine is at temperature, set the breasts in the basket and air-fry undisturbed for 10 minutes.
4. Top the chicken breasts with the apple slices, then the cheese. Air-fry undisturbed for 2 minutes, or until the cheese is melty and bubbling.
5. Use a nonstick-safe spatula and kitchen tongs, for balance, to transfer the breasts to a cutting board. Set the rolls in the basket and air-fry for 1 minute to warm through. (Putting them in the machine without splitting them keeps the insides very soft while the outside gets a little crunchy.)
6. Transfer the rolls to the cutting board. Split them open lengthwise, then spread 1 teaspoon mustard on each cut side. Set a prepared chicken breast on the bottom of a roll and close with its top, repeating as necessary to make additional sandwiches. Serve warm.

Turkey Burgers

Servings: 3
Cooking Time: 23 Minutes

Ingredients:
- 1 pound 2 ounces Ground turkey
- 6 tablespoons Frozen chopped spinach, thawed and squeezed dry
- 3 tablespoons Plain panko bread crumbs (gluten-free, if a concern)
- 1 tablespoon Dijon mustard (gluten-free, if a concern)
- 1½ teaspoons Minced garlic
- ¾ teaspoon Table salt
- ¾ teaspoon Ground black pepper
- Olive oil spray
- 3 Kaiser rolls (gluten-free, if a concern), split open

Directions:

1. Preheat the air fryer to 375°F .
2. Gently mix the ground turkey, spinach, bread crumbs, mustard, garlic, salt, and pepper in a large bowl until well combined, trying to keep some of the fibers of the ground turkey intact. Form into two 5-inch-wide patties for the small batch, three 5-inch patties for the medium batch, or four 5-inch patties for the large. Coat each side of the patties with olive oil spray.
3. Set the patties in in the basket in one layer and air-fry undisturbed for 20 minutes, or until an instant-read meat thermometer inserted into the center of a burger registers 165°F. You may need to add 2 minutes to the cooking time if the air fryer is at 360°F.
4. Use a nonstick-safe spatula, and perhaps a flatware fork for balance, to transfer the burgers to a cutting board. Set the buns cut side down in the basket in one layer (working in batches as necessary) and air-fry for 1 minute, to toast a bit and warm up. Serve the burgers warm in the buns.

Reuben Sandwiches

Servings: 2

Cooking Time: 11 Minutes

Ingredients:

- ½ pound Sliced deli corned beef
- 4 teaspoons Regular or low-fat mayonnaise (not fat-free)
- 4 Rye bread slices
- 2 tablespoons plus 2 teaspoons Russian dressing
- ½ cup Purchased sauerkraut, squeezed by the handful over the sink to get rid of excess moisture
- 2 ounces (2 to 4 slices) Swiss cheese slices (optional)

Directions:

1. Set the corned beef in the basket, slip the basket into the machine, and heat the air fryer to 400°F. Air-fry undisturbed for 3 minutes from the time the basket is put in the machine, just to warm up the meat.

2. Use kitchen tongs to transfer the corned beef to a cutting board. Spread 1 teaspoon mayonnaise on one side of each slice of rye bread, rubbing the mayonnaise into the bread with a small flatware knife.

3. Place the bread slices mayonnaise side down on a cutting board. Spread the Russian dressing over the "dry" side of each slice. For one sandwich, top one slice of bread with the corned beef, sauerkraut, and cheese (if using). For two sandwiches, top two slices of bread each with half of the corned beef, sauerkraut, and cheese (if using). Close the sandwiches with the remaining bread, setting it mayonnaise side up on top.

4. Set the sandwich(es) in the basket and air-fry undisturbed for 8 minutes, or until browned and crunchy.

5. Use a nonstick-safe spatula, and perhaps a flatware fork for balance, to transfer the sandwich(es) to a cutting board. Cool for 2 or 3 minutes before slicing in half and serving.

Asian Glazed Meatballs

Servings: 4

Cooking Time: 10 Minutes

Ingredients:

- 1 large shallot, finely chopped
- 2 cloves garlic, minced
- 1 tablespoon grated fresh ginger
- 2 teaspoons fresh thyme, finely chopped
- 1½ cups brown mushrooms, very finely chopped (a food processor works well here)
- 2 tablespoons soy sauce
- freshly ground black pepper
- 1 pound ground beef
- ½ pound ground pork
- 3 egg yolks
- 1 cup Thai sweet chili sauce (spring roll sauce)
- ¼ cup toasted sesame seeds
- 2 scallions, sliced

Directions:

1. Combine the shallot, garlic, ginger, thyme, mushrooms, soy sauce, freshly ground black pepper, ground beef and pork, and egg yolks in a bowl and mix the ingredients together. Gently

shape the mixture into 24 balls, about the size of a golf ball.

2. Preheat the air fryer to 380°F.

3. Working in batches, air-fry the meatballs for 8 minutes, turning the meatballs over halfway through the cooking time. Drizzle some of the Thai sweet chili sauce on top of each meatball and return the basket to the air fryer, air-frying for another 2 minutes. Reserve the remaining Thai sweet chili sauce for serving.

4. As soon as the meatballs are done, sprinkle with toasted sesame seeds and transfer them to a serving platter. Scatter the scallions around and serve warm.

RECIPE INDEX

Shrimp Po'boy With Remoulade Sauce 118
Shrimp Teriyaki 117
Smokehouse-style Beef Ribs 23
Southwest Gluten-free Turkey Meatloaf 28
Spaghetti Squash And Kale Fritters With
Pomodoro Sauce 93
Spicy Chicken And Pepper Jack Cheese Bites 51
Spicy Sesame Tempeh Slaw With Peanut
Dressing 105
Spicy Vegetable And Tofu Shake Fry 99
Steakhouse Burgers With Red Onion Compote
19
Steamboat Shrimp Salad 55
Strawberry Bread 66
Struffoli 80
Stuffed Onions 55
Stuffed Zucchini Boats 105
Sweet And Spicy Pumpkin Scones 64
Sweet Potato-cinnamon Toast 66
Sweet Potato–wrapped Shrimp 108
Sweet-and-salty Pretzels 50
Sweet-and-sour Chicken 35

T

Tandoori Cauliflower 56
Tandoori Chicken Legs 30

Taquitos 37
Teriyaki Chicken Drumsticks 33
Thai Peanut Veggie Burgers 91
Thai-style Pork Sliders 127
Thanksgiving Turkey Sandwiches 123
Tilapia Teriyaki 116
Tortilla Crusted Chicken Breast 37
Turkey Burgers 129

V

Vegetable Couscous 96
Vegetable Hand Pies 103
Veggie Fried Rice 98
Vietnamese Beef Lettuce Wraps 18

W

White Bean Veggie Burgers 128
White Chocolate Cranberry Blondies 85
Wild Blueberry Sweet Empanadas 83

Z

Zesty London Broil 17
Zucchini Boats With Ham And Cheese 54
Zucchini Fries 61
Zucchini Walnut Bread 70

Printed by Libri Plureos GmbH in Hamburg,
Germany